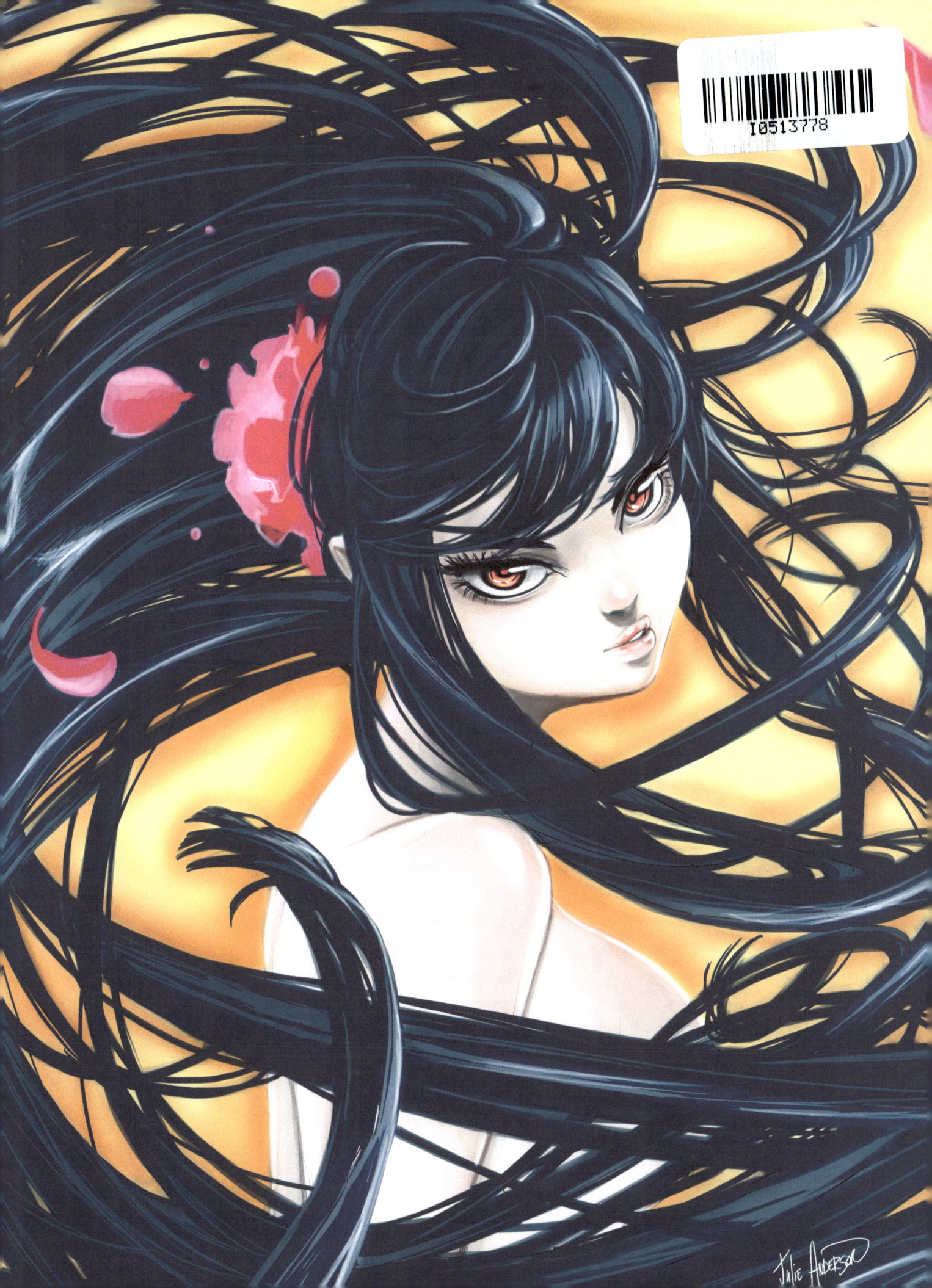

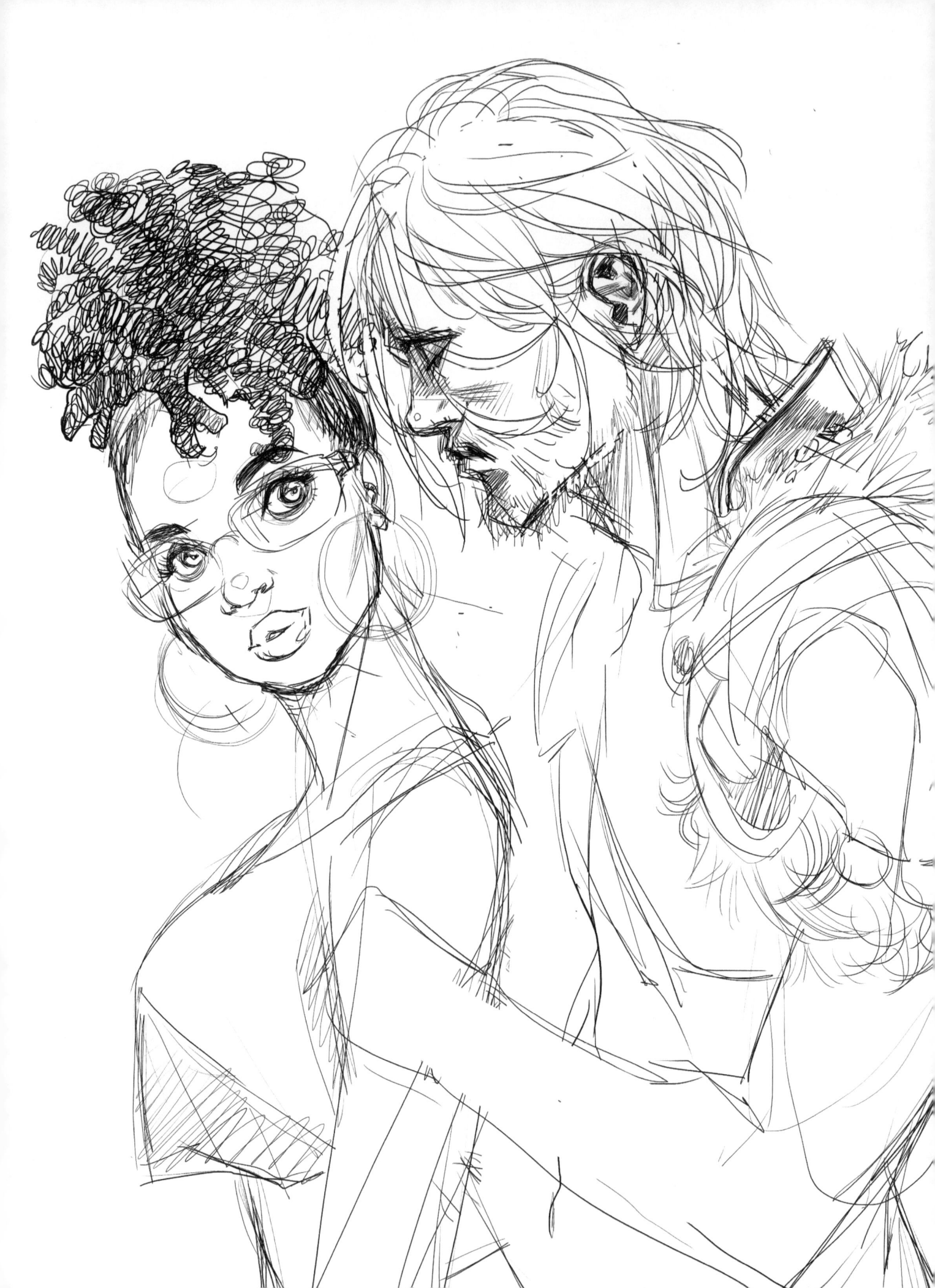

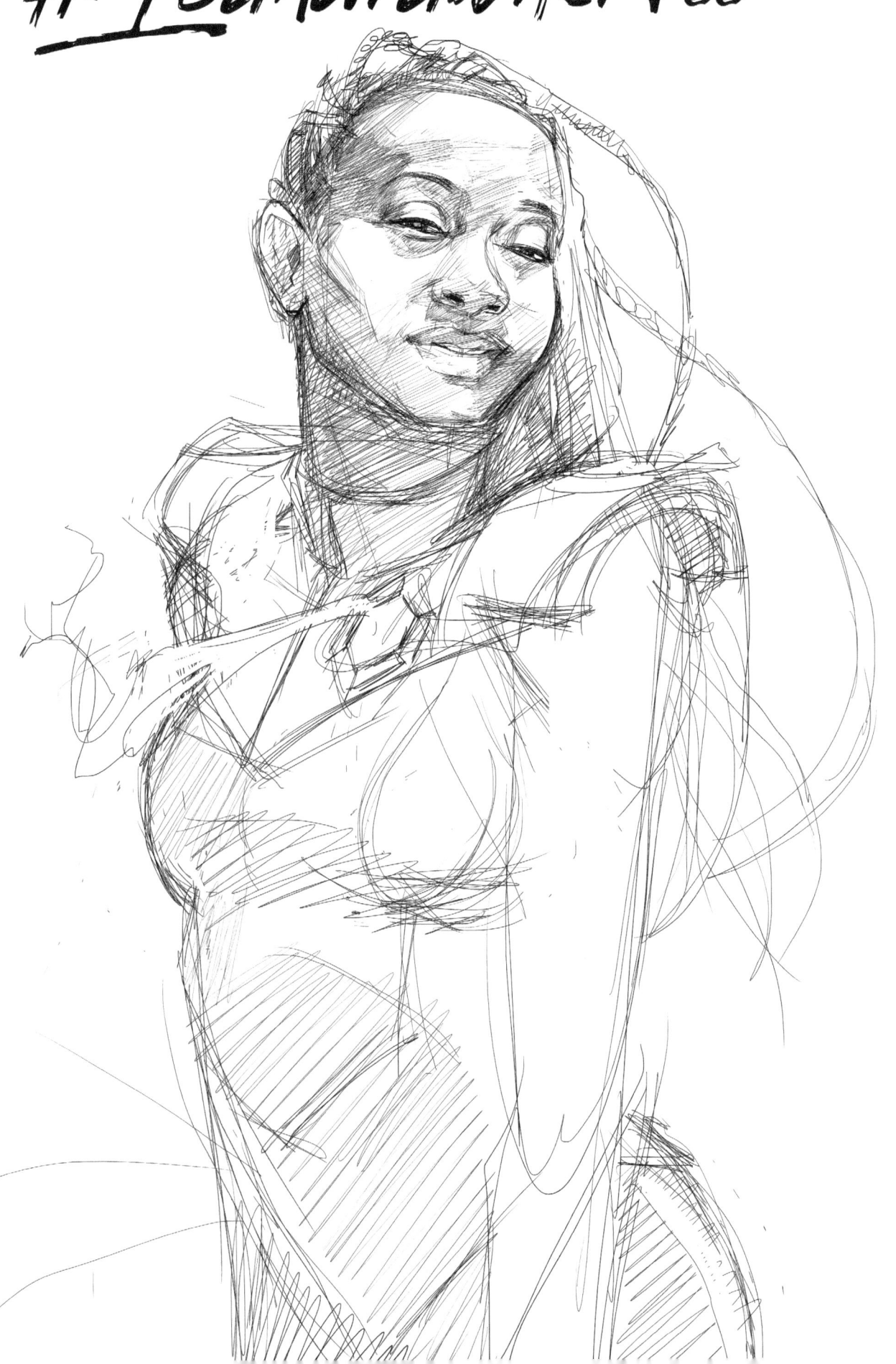

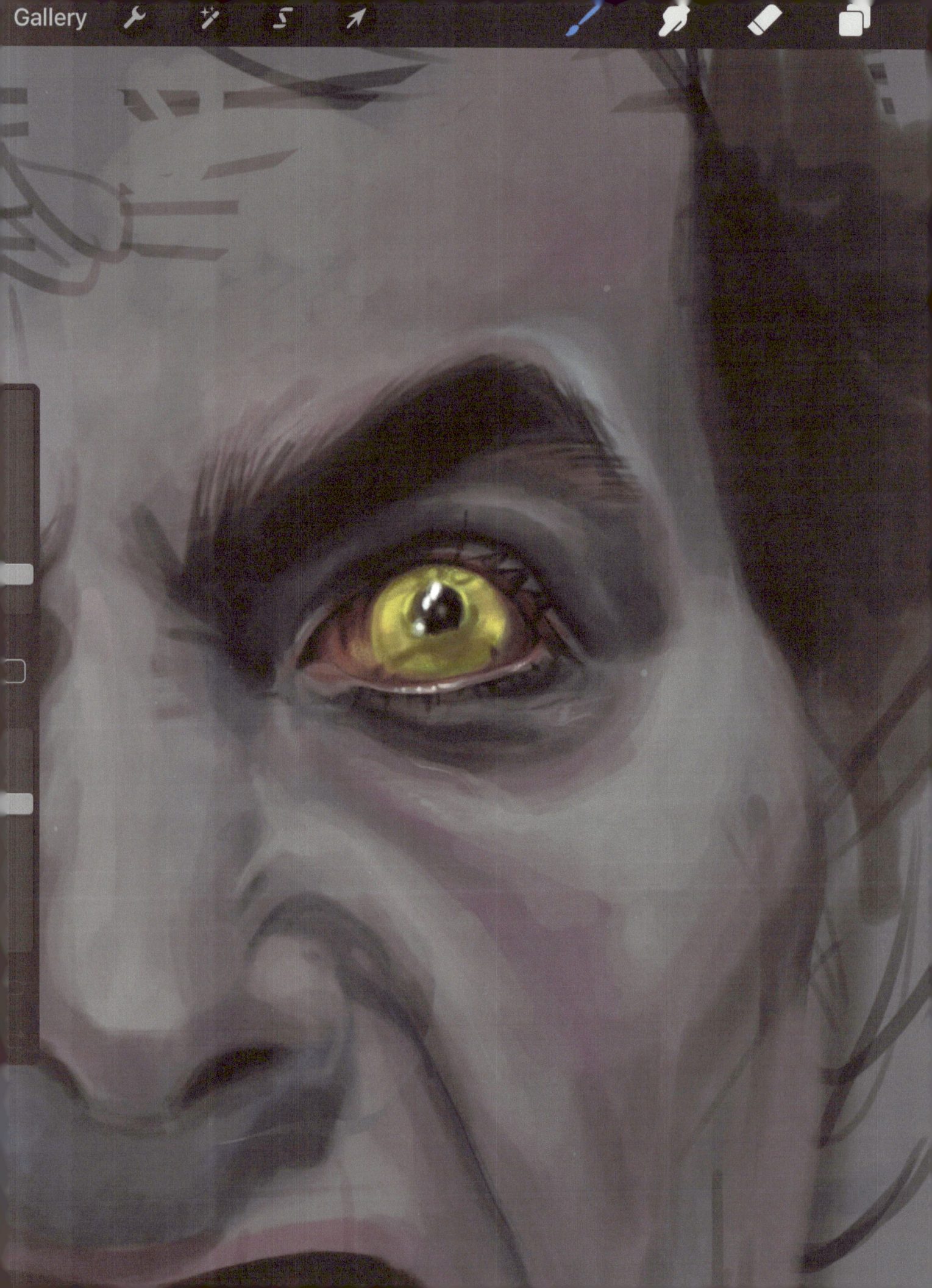

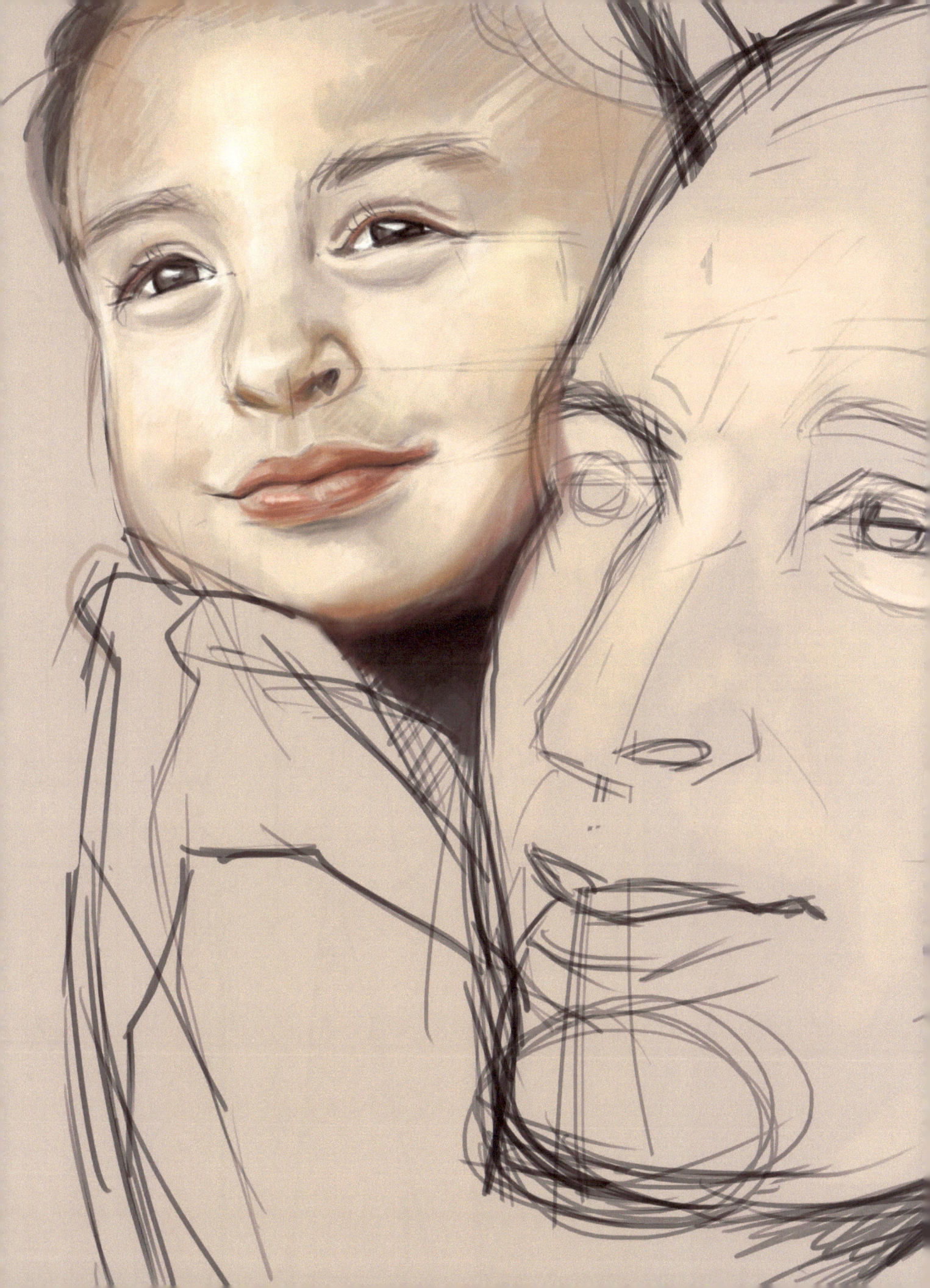

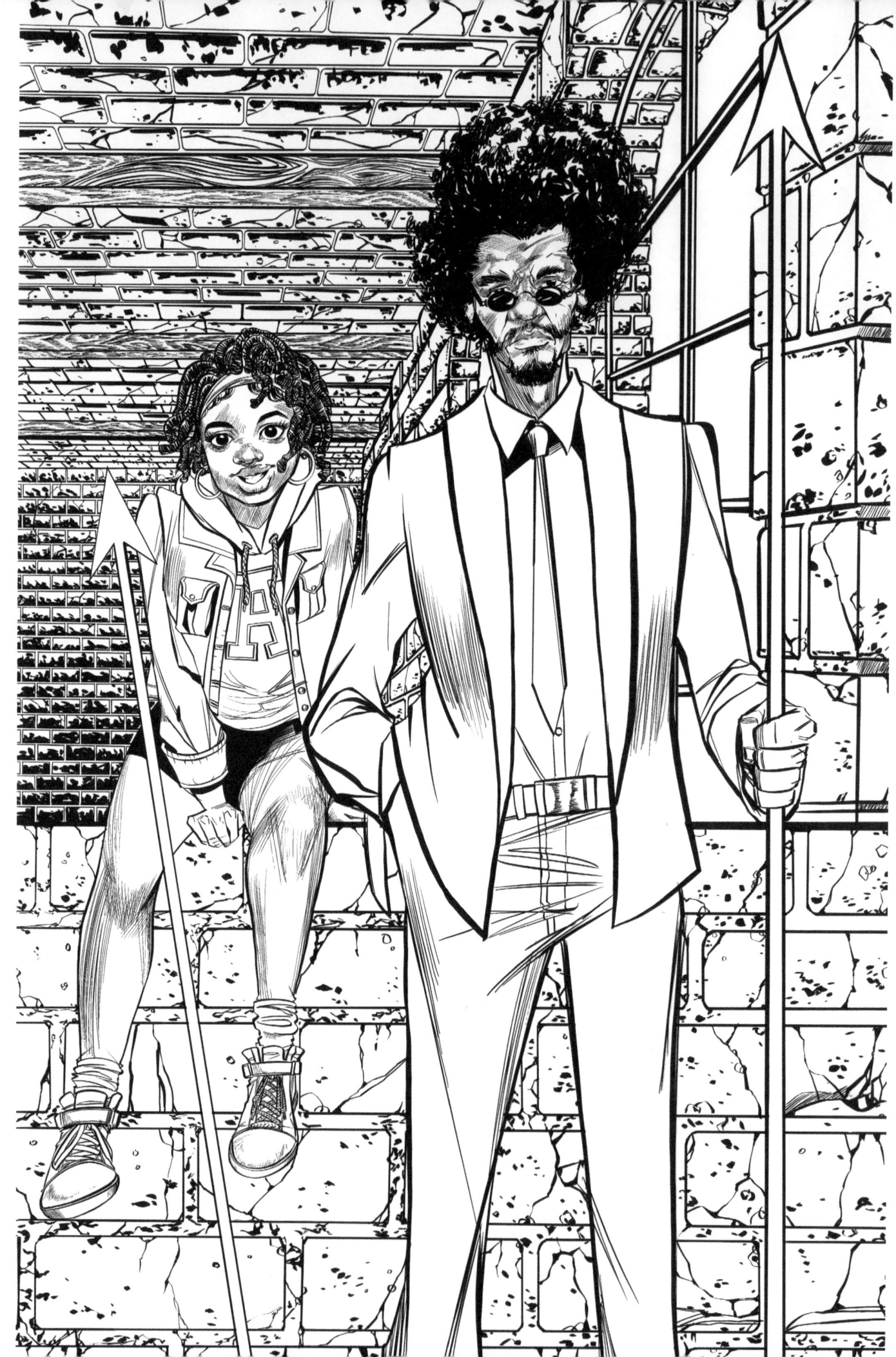

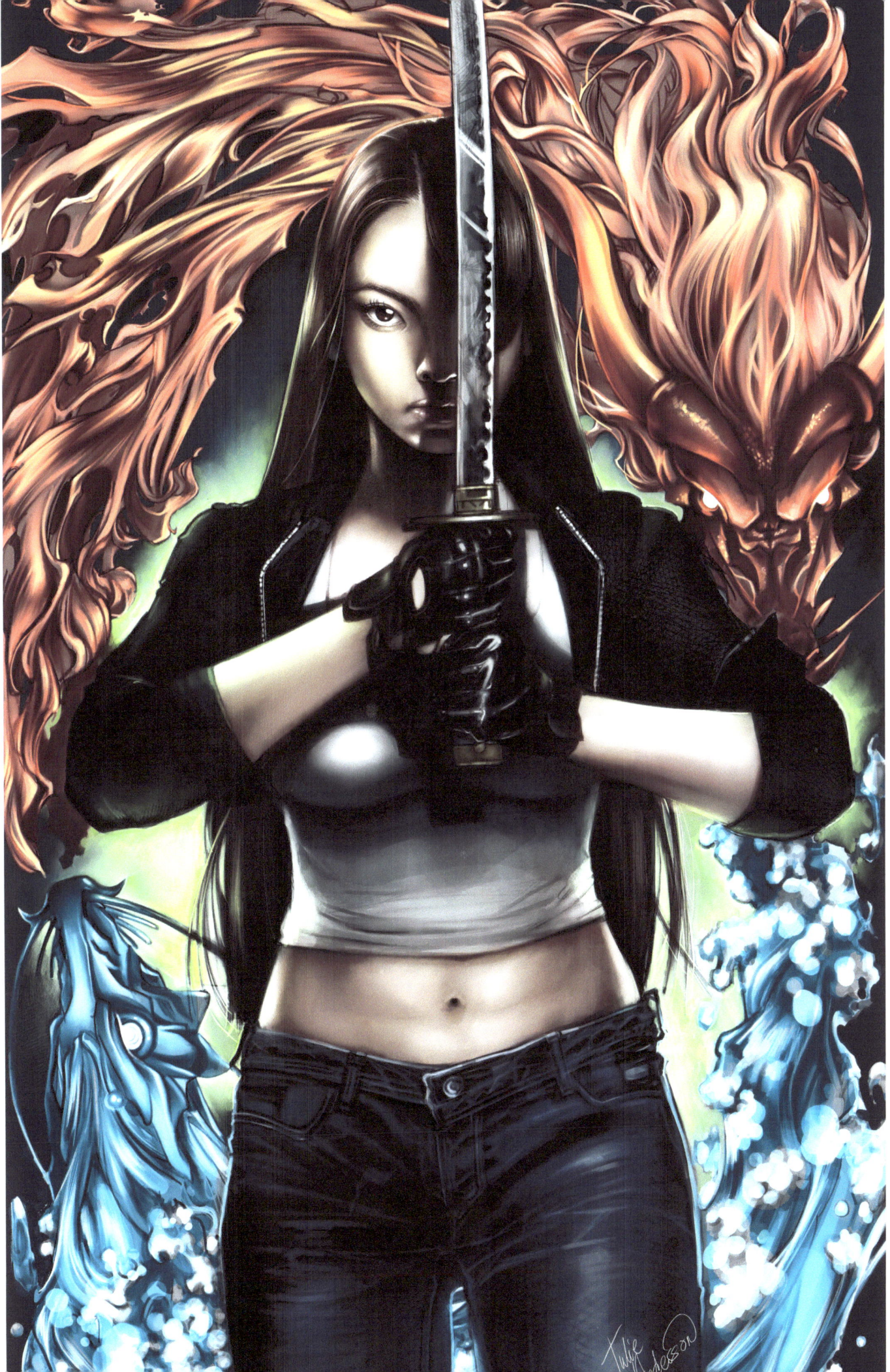

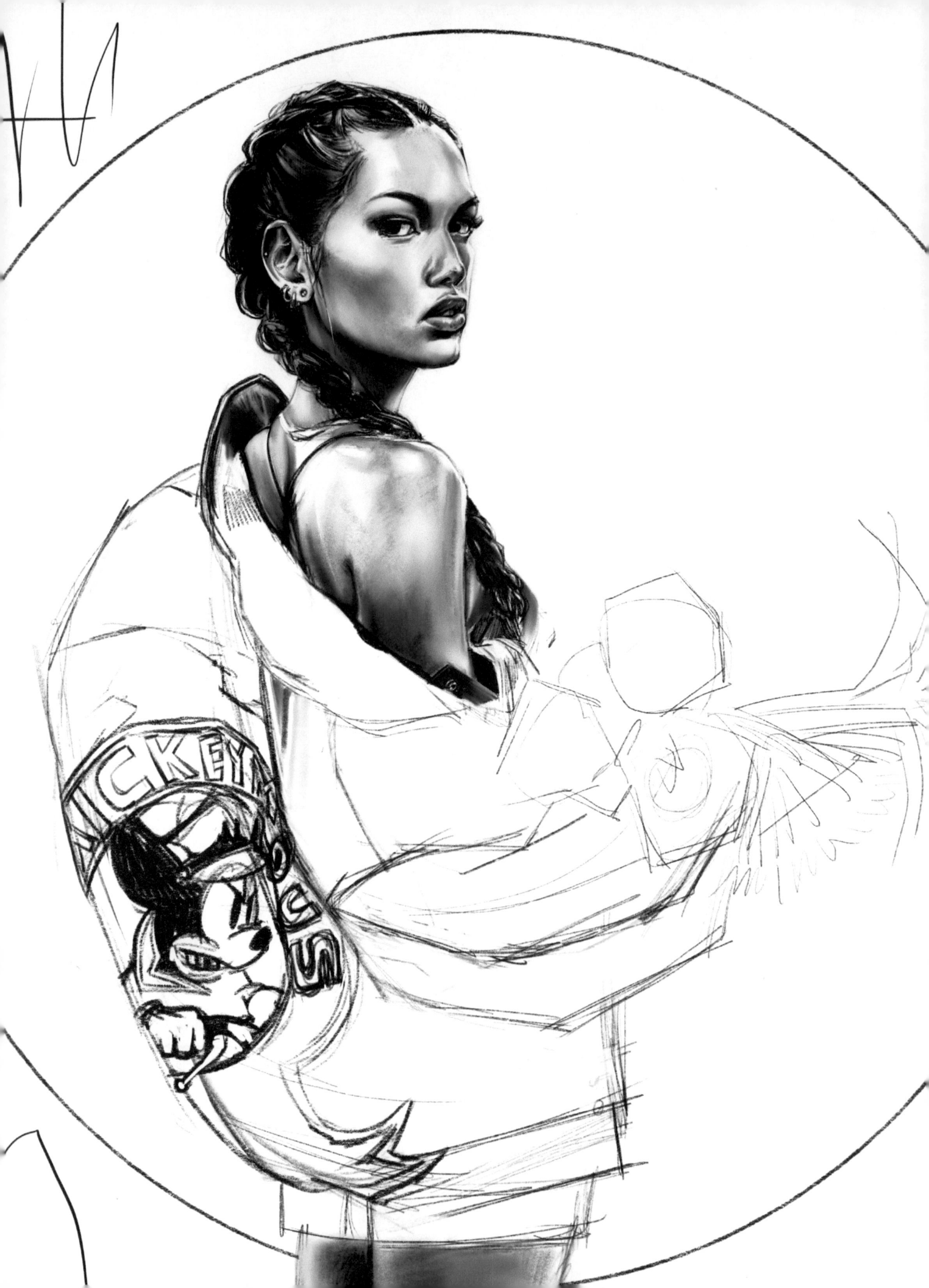

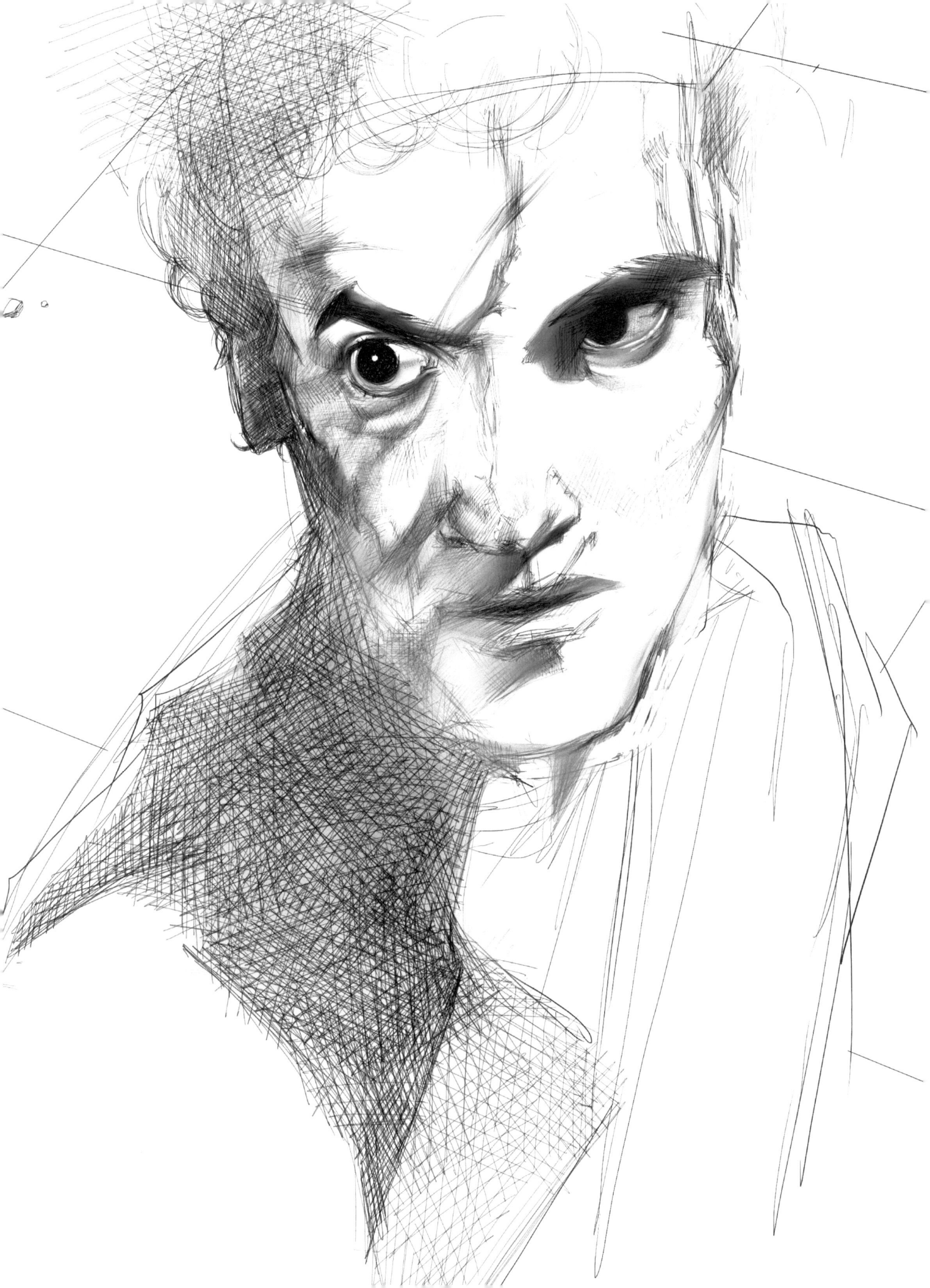

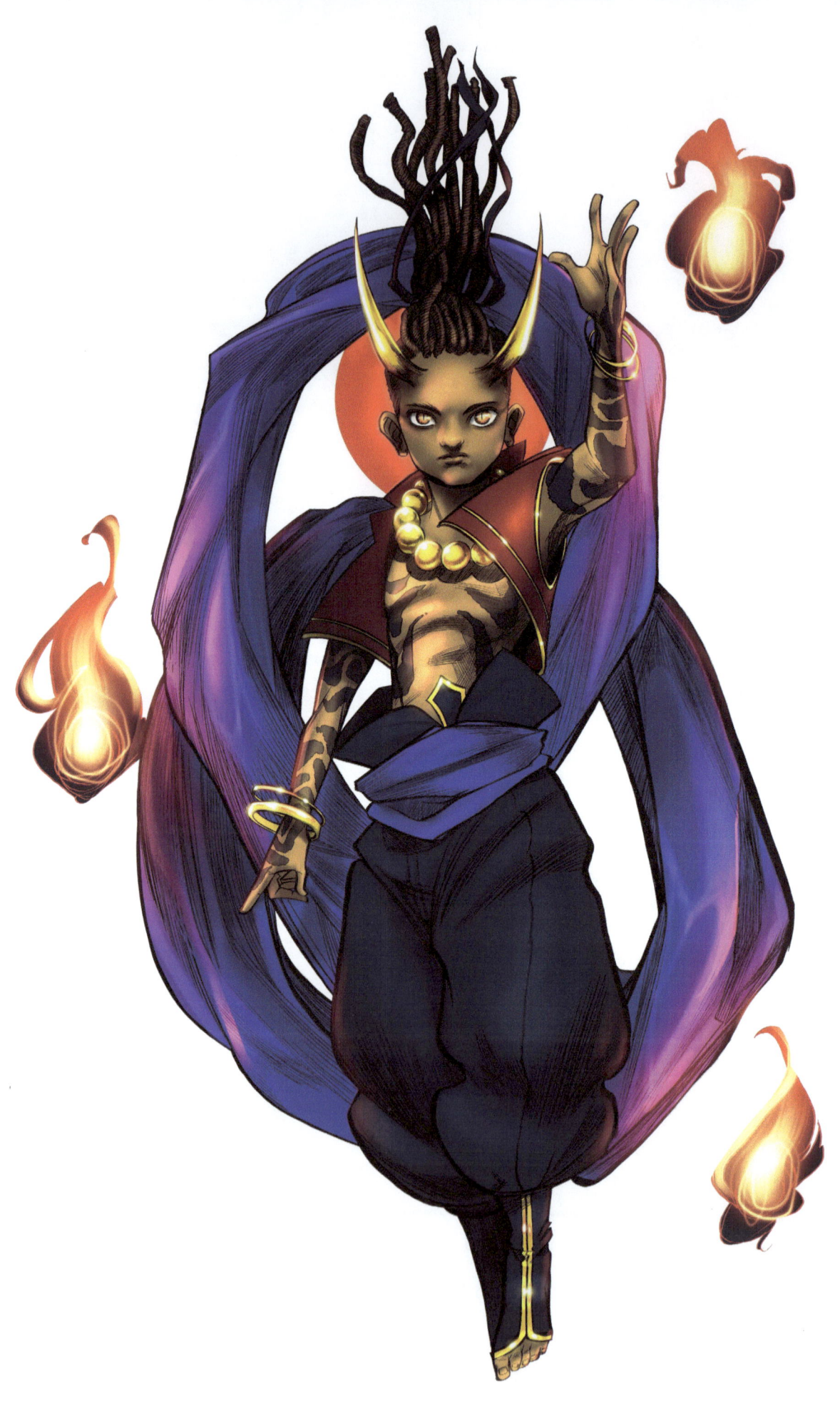

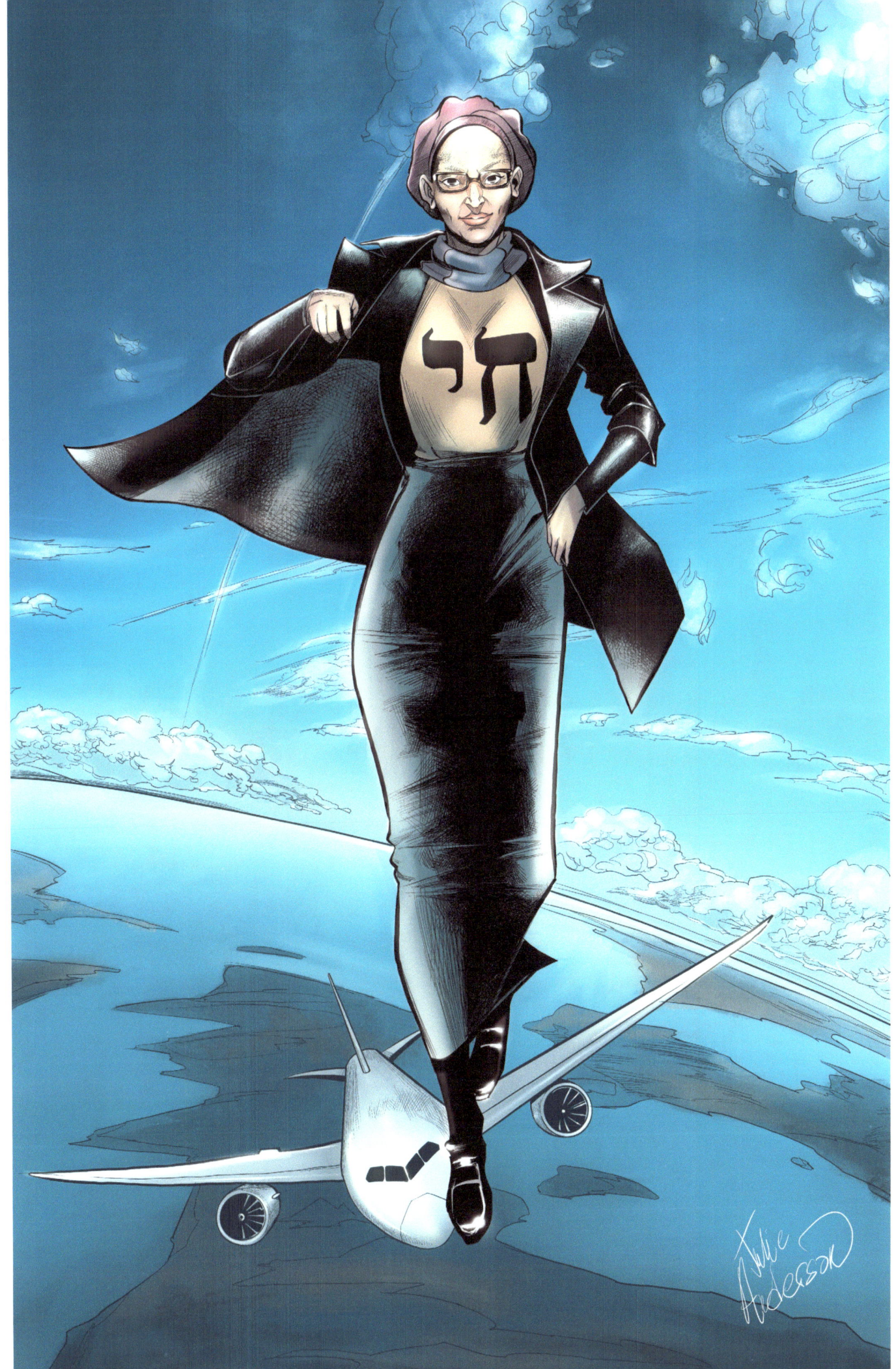

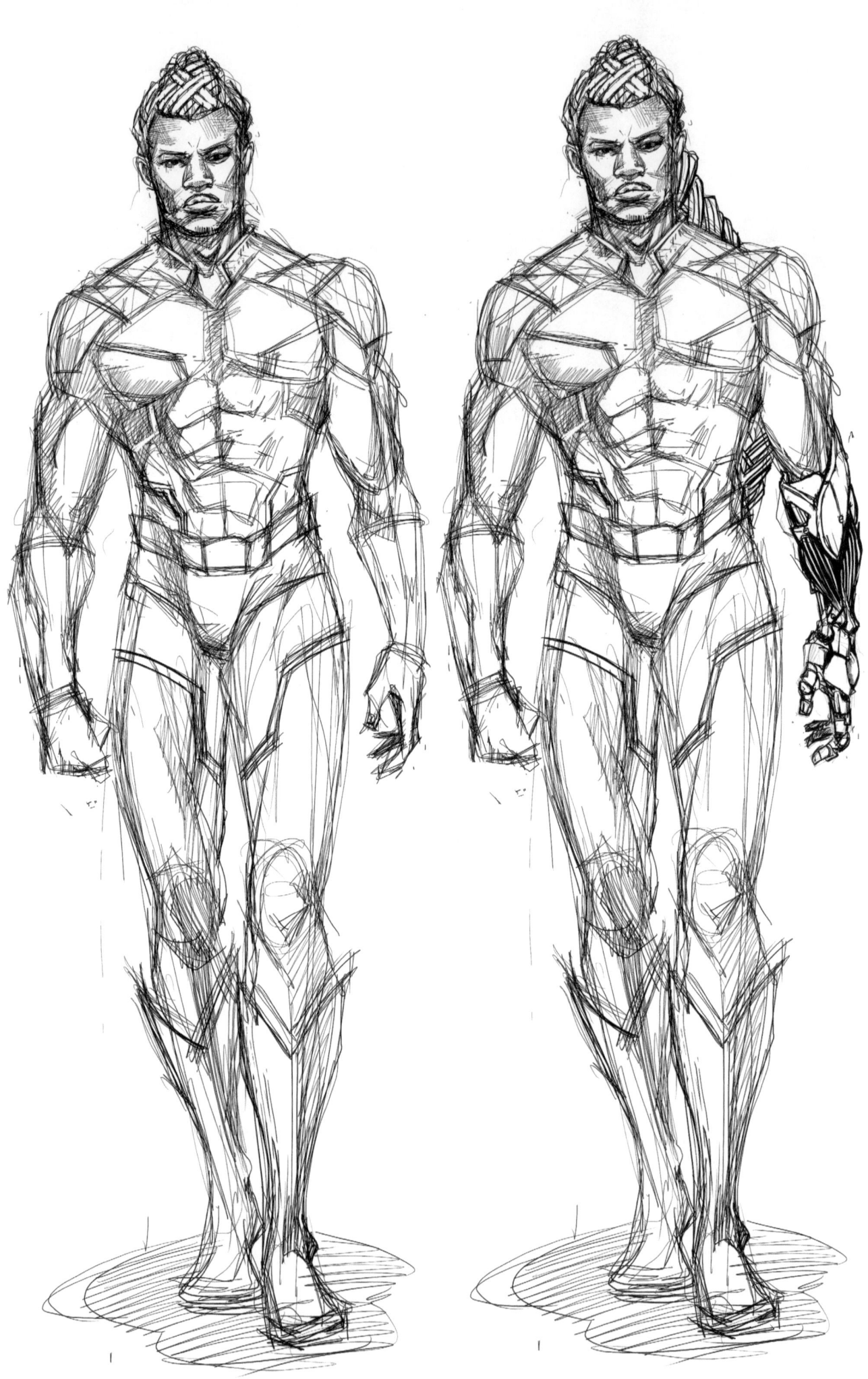

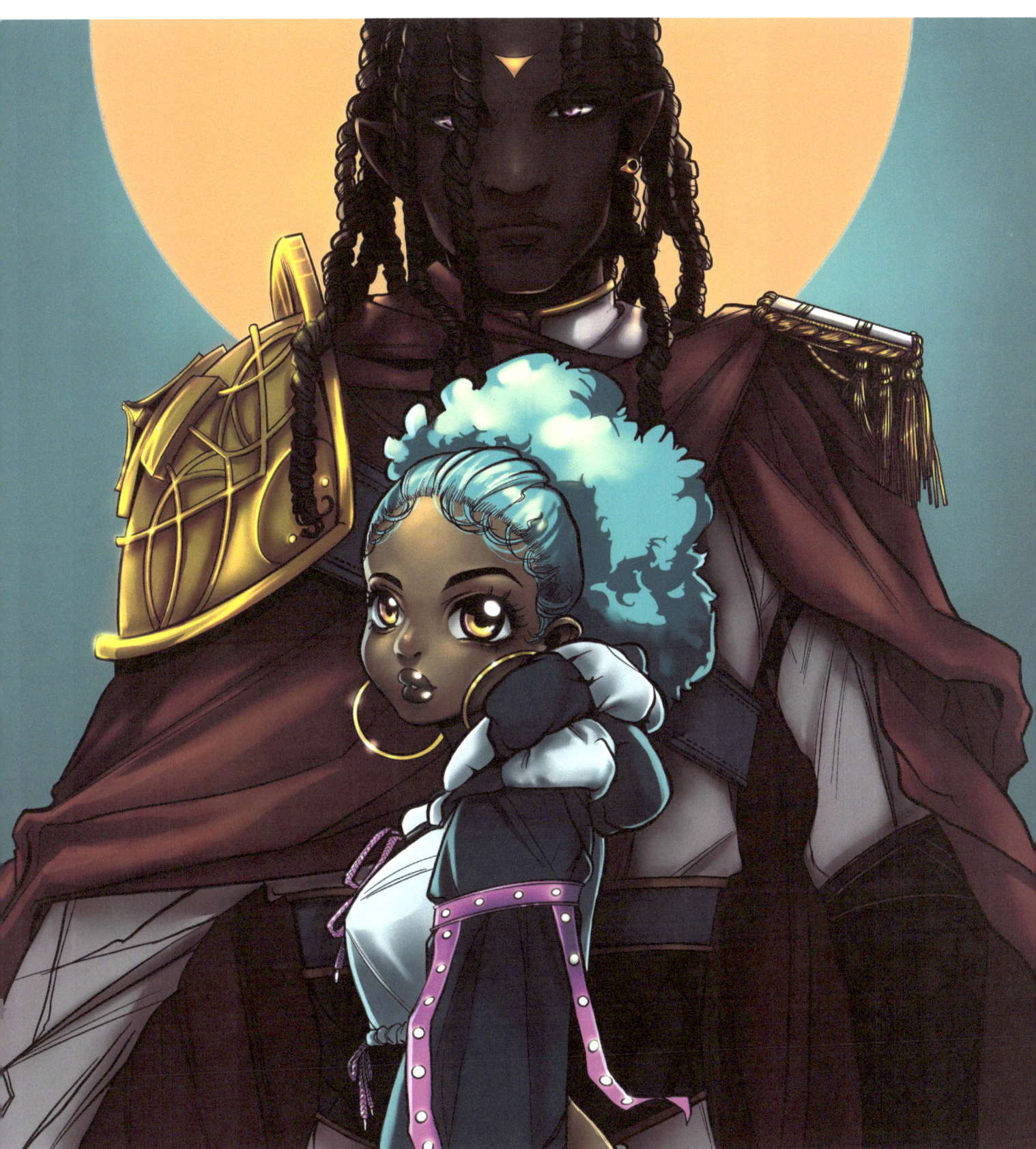

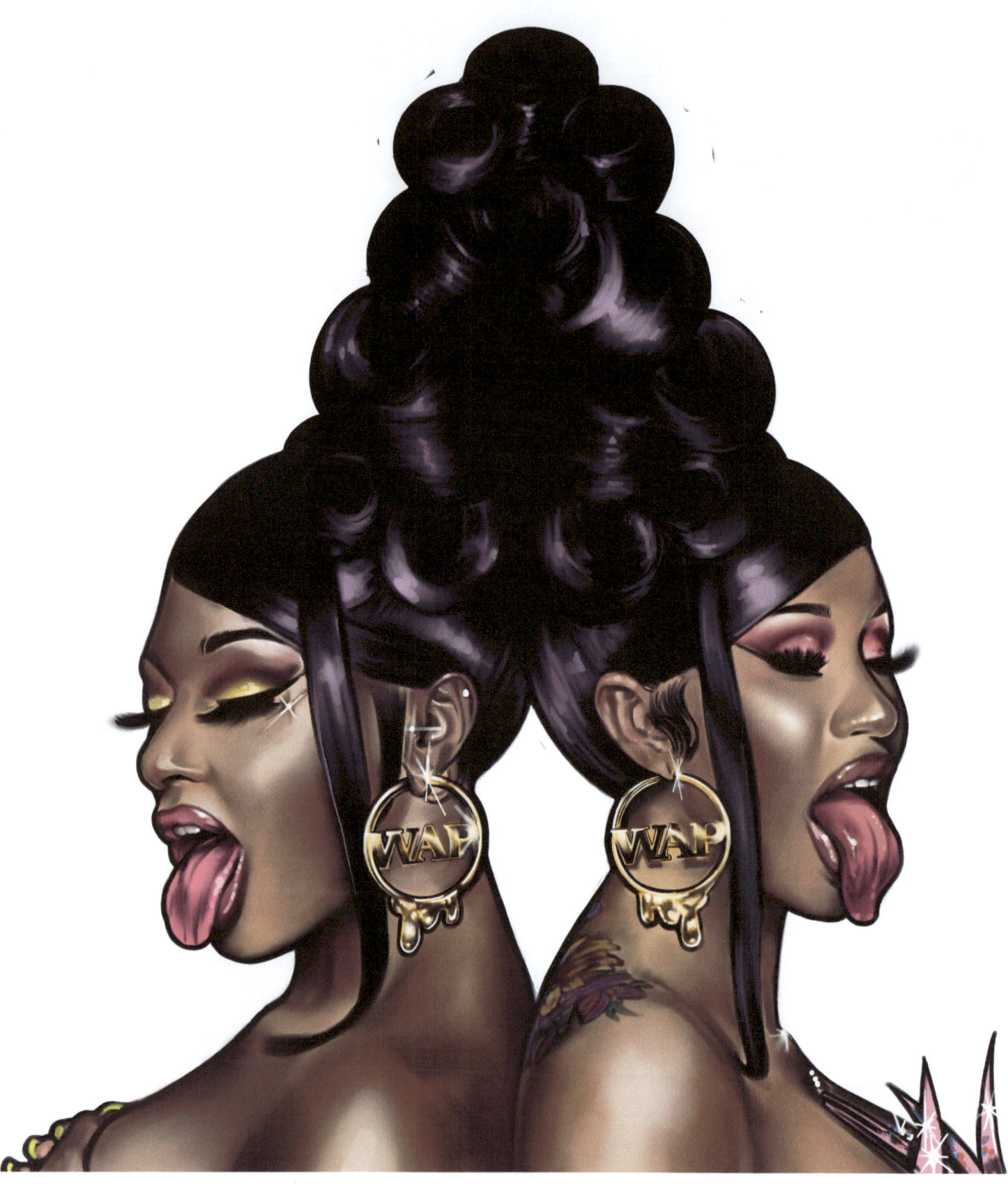

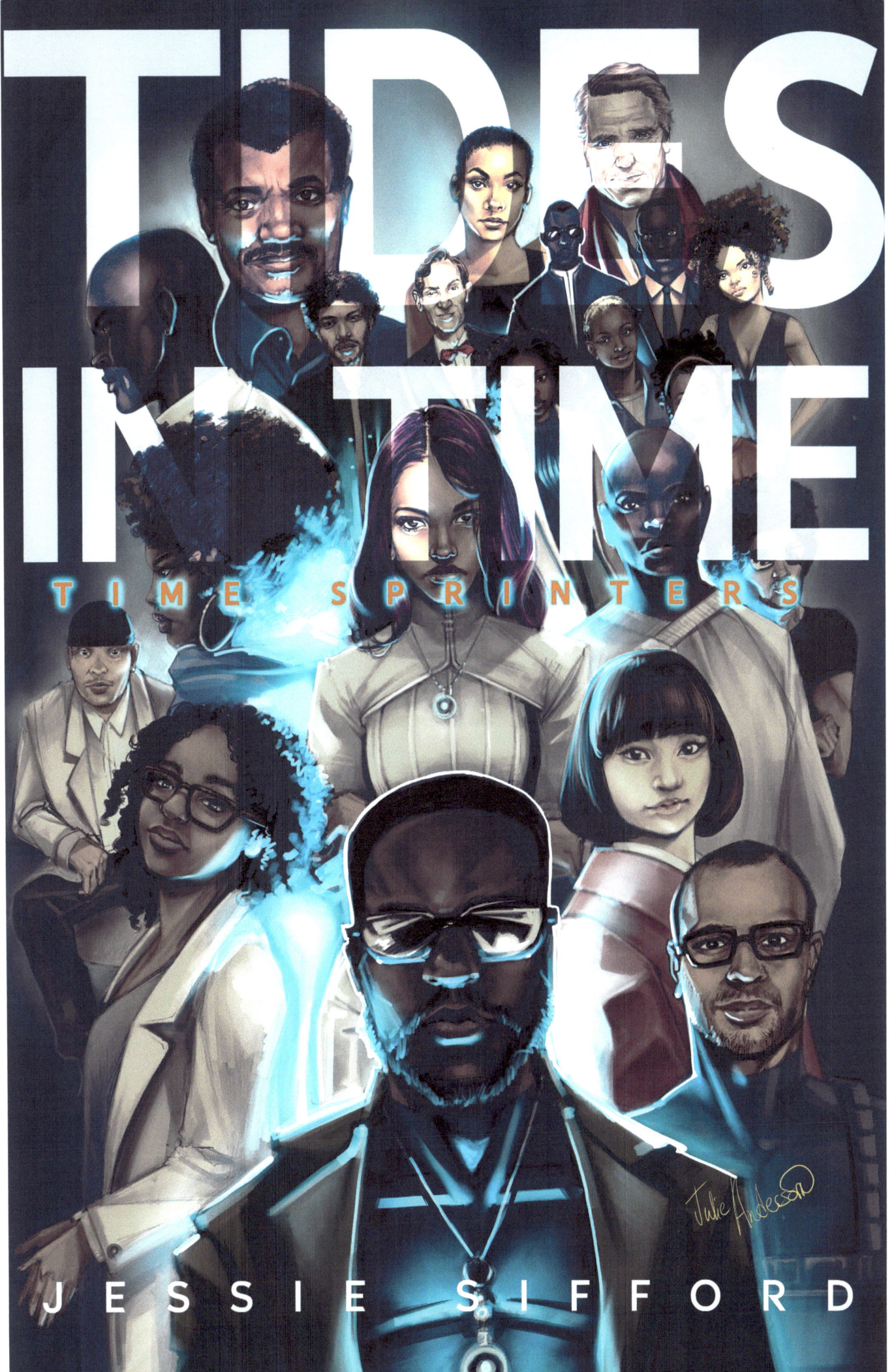

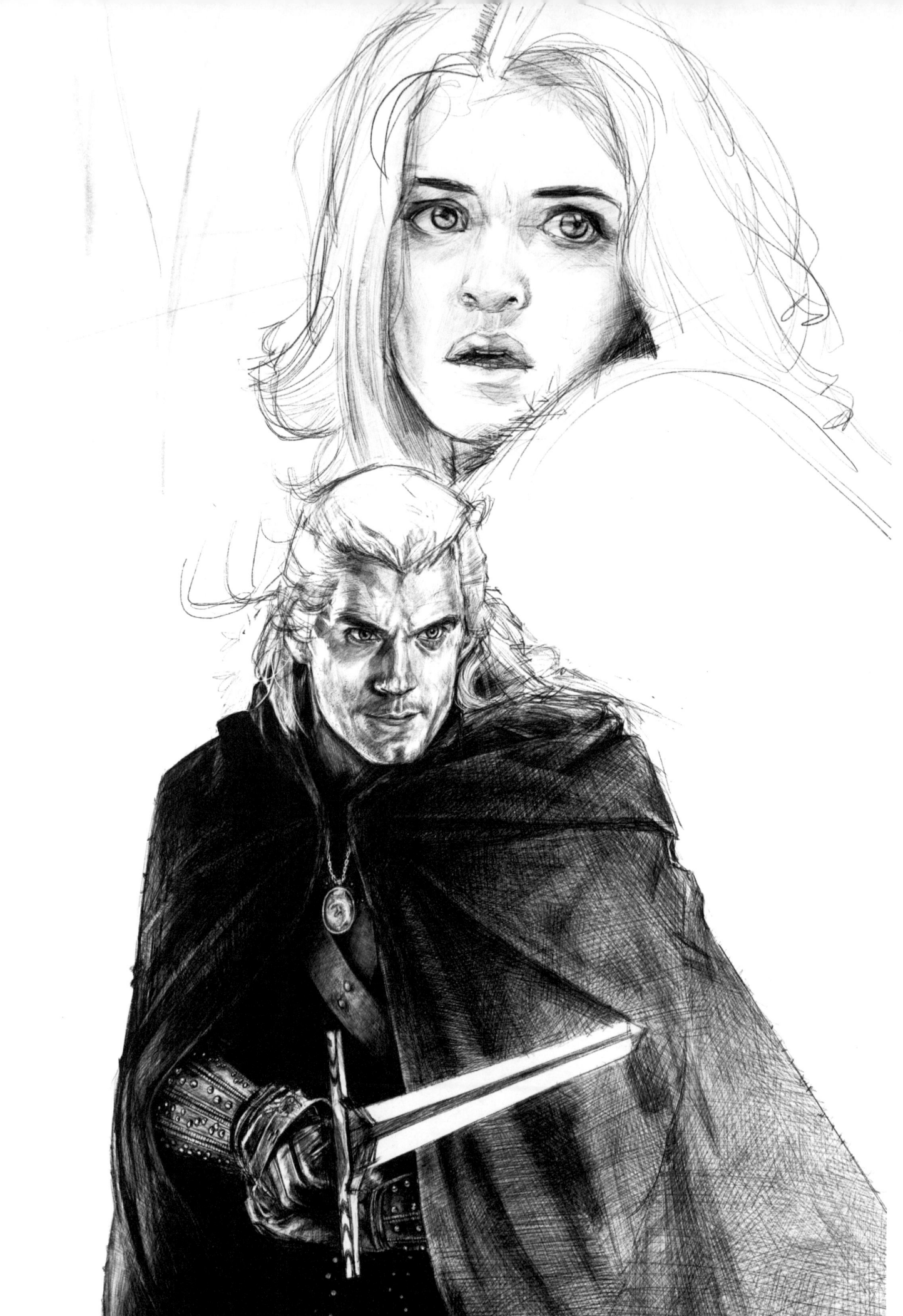

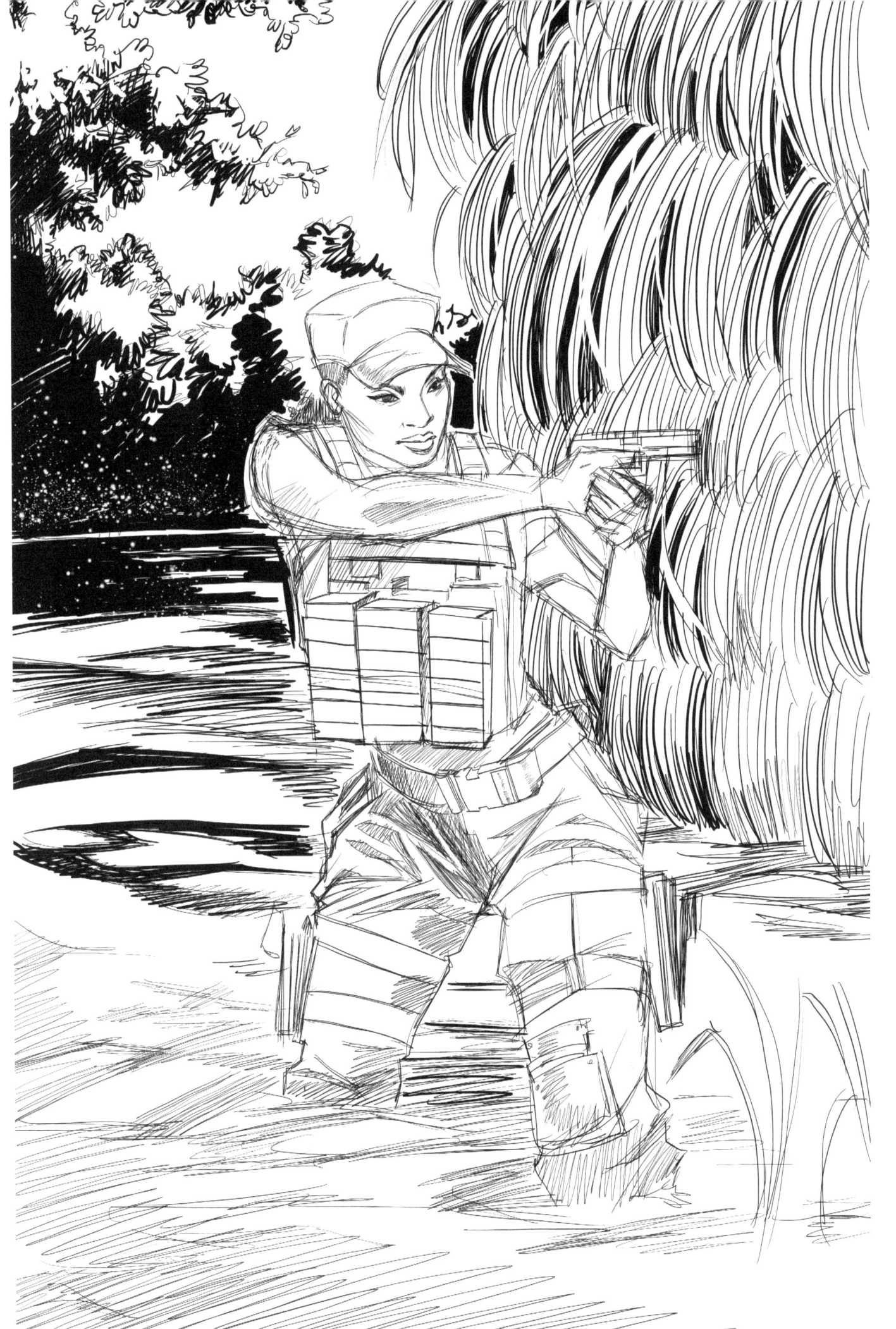

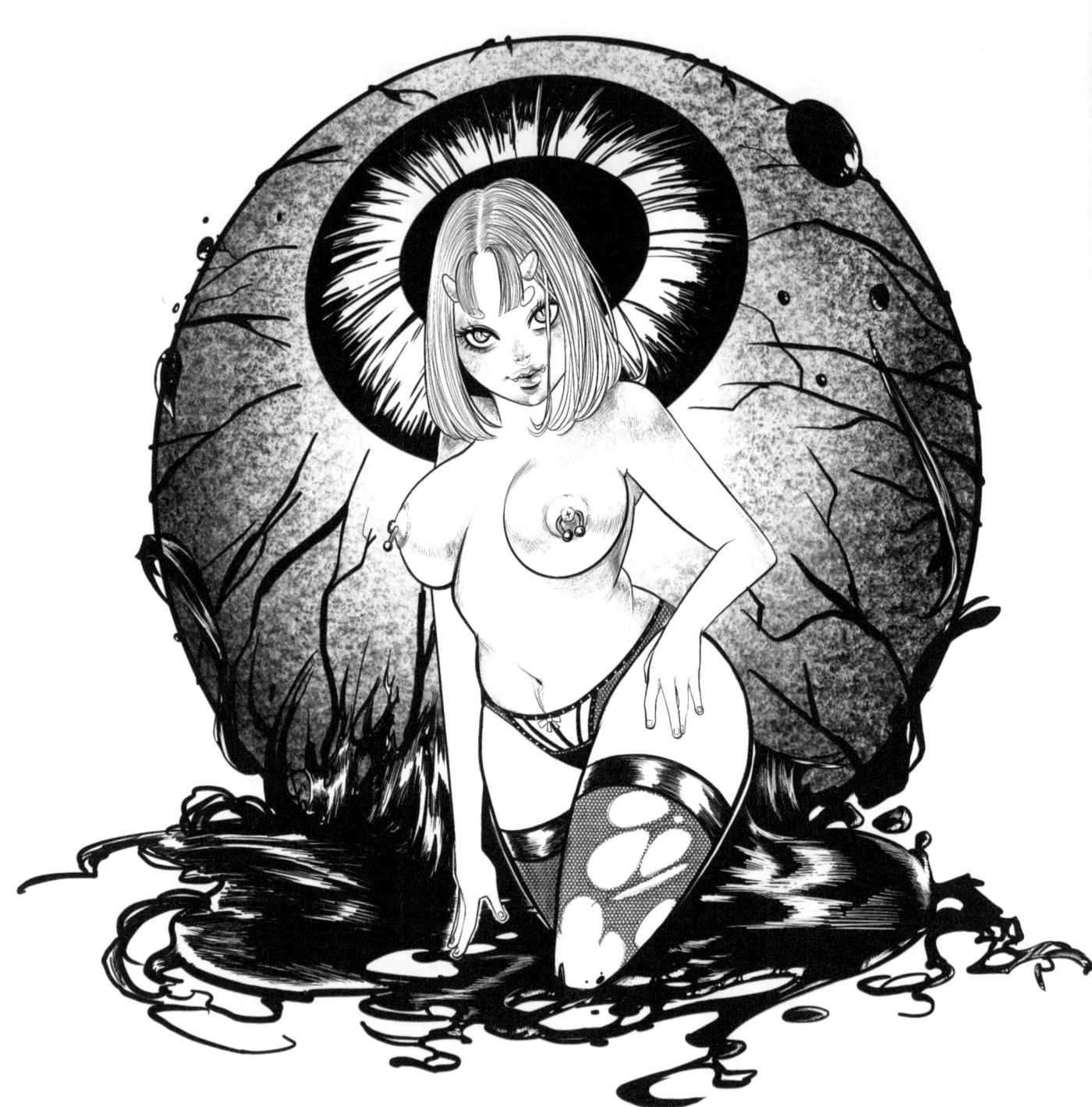

Film Noir

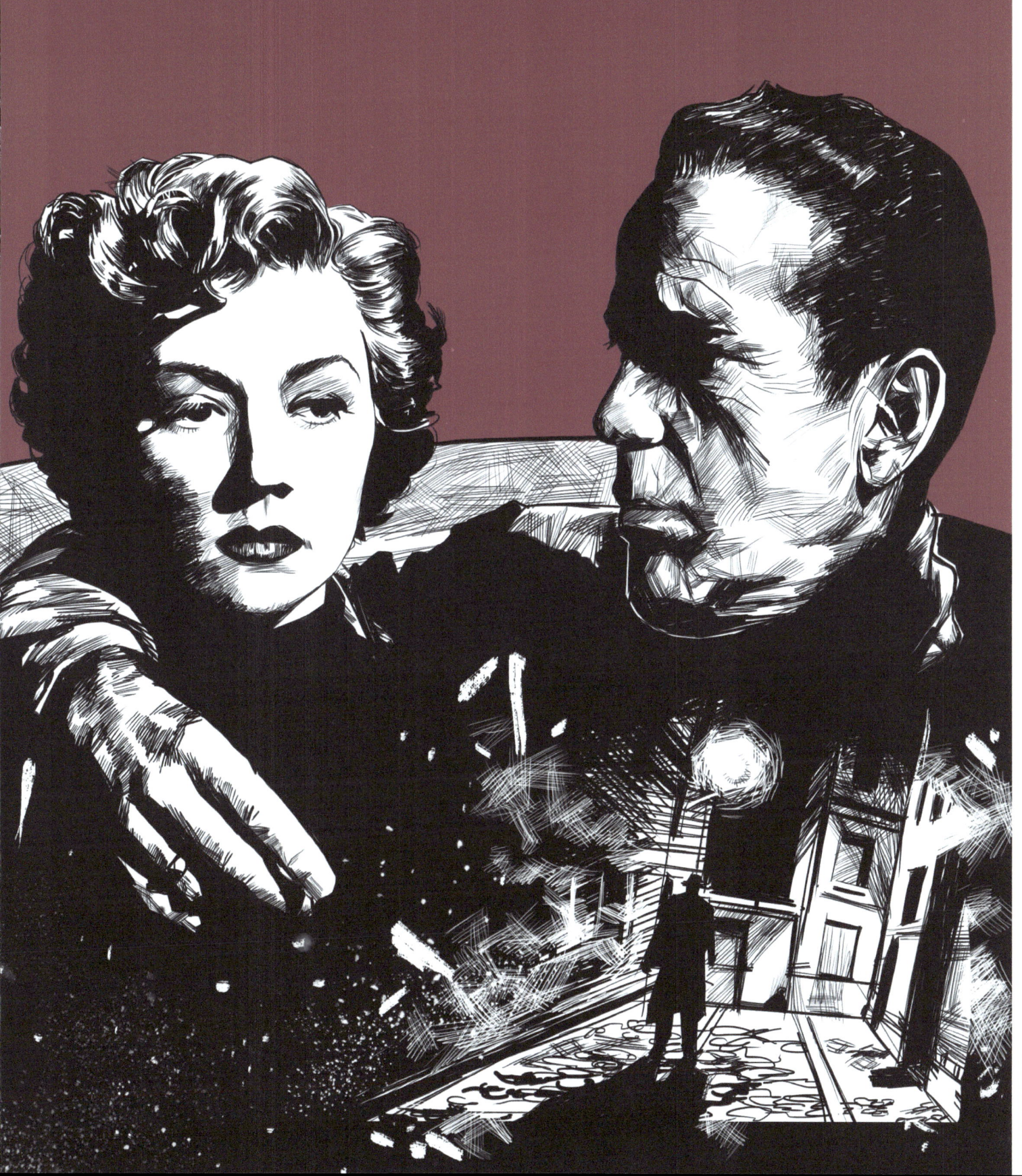

Film noir contains a set of archetypical characters:
- the hero is often an outlaw, a misfit, or a jaded gumshoe (all usually emotionally perturbed)

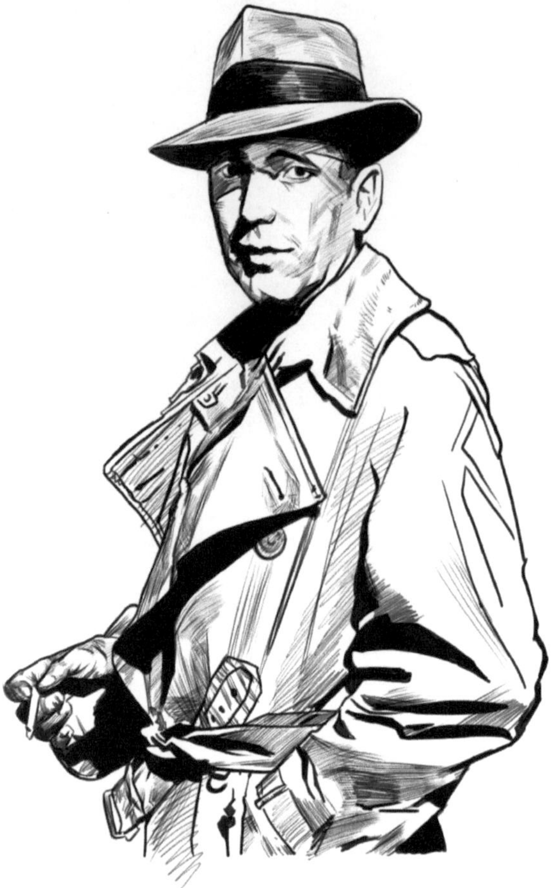

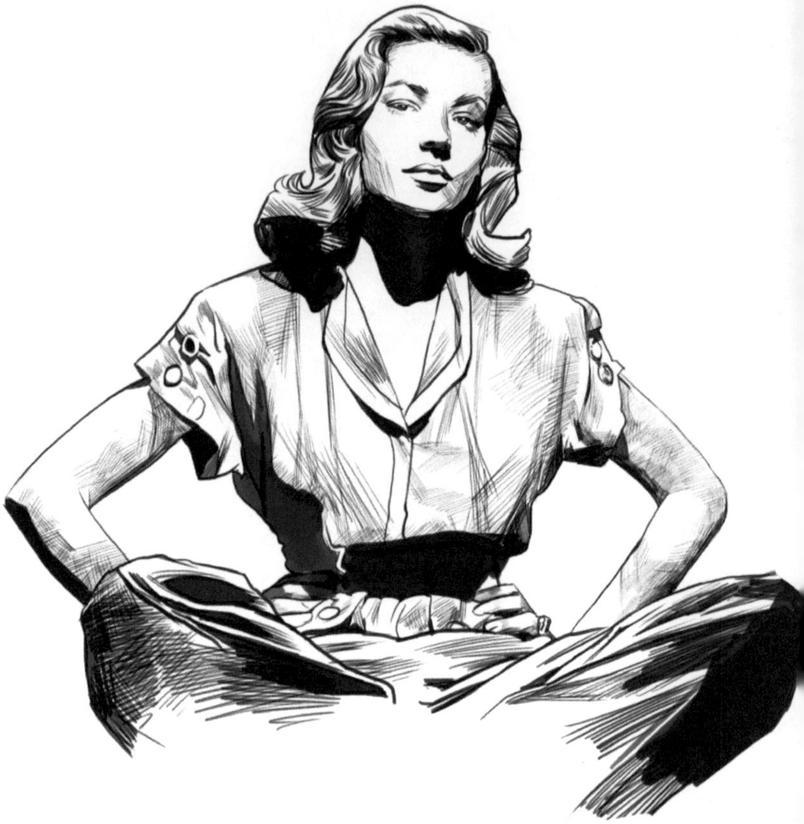

- femme fatale—a mysterious woman whose seductive behavior foreshadows the hero's inevitable doom

- bad girl—dispensable and often abused woman

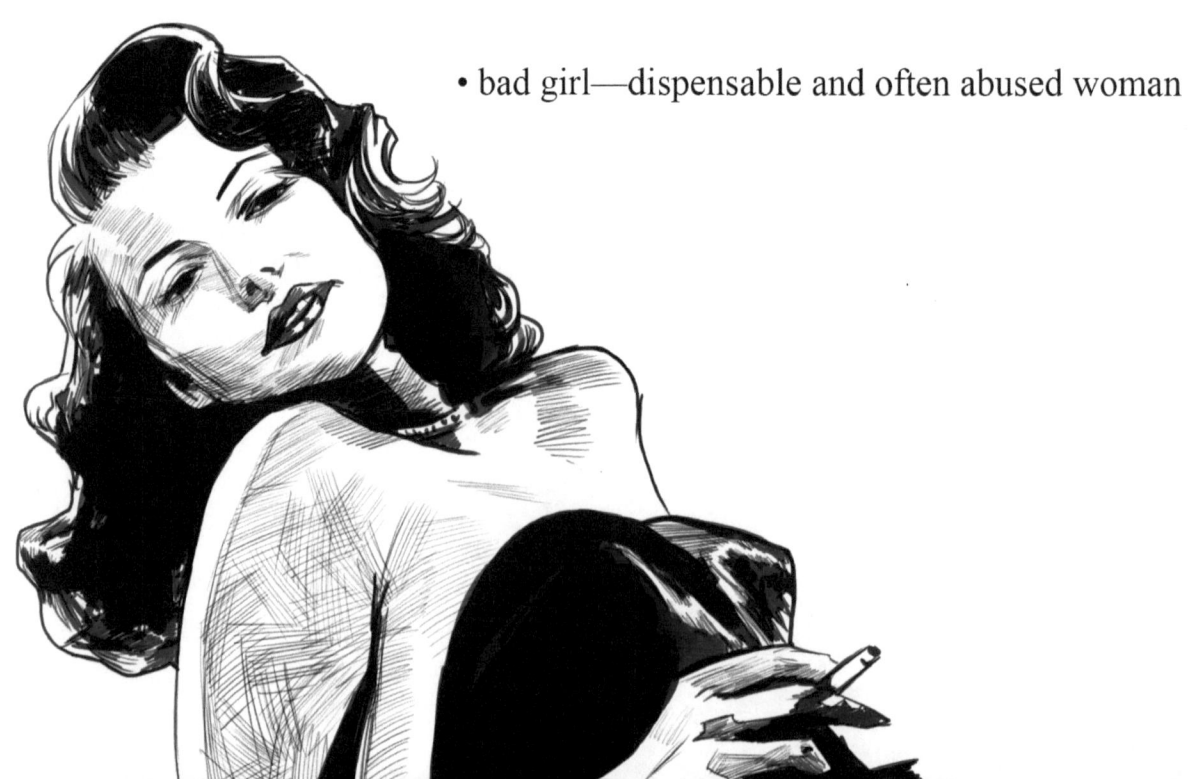

The stylishly murky settings of The Maltese Falcon (dir. John Huston, 1941) and This Gun For Hire (dir. Frank Tuttle, 1942) anticipate the more pessimistic outlook of such film noir classics as Double Indemnity (dir. Billy Wilder, 1944) and Out of the Past (dir. Jaques Tourneur, 1947).

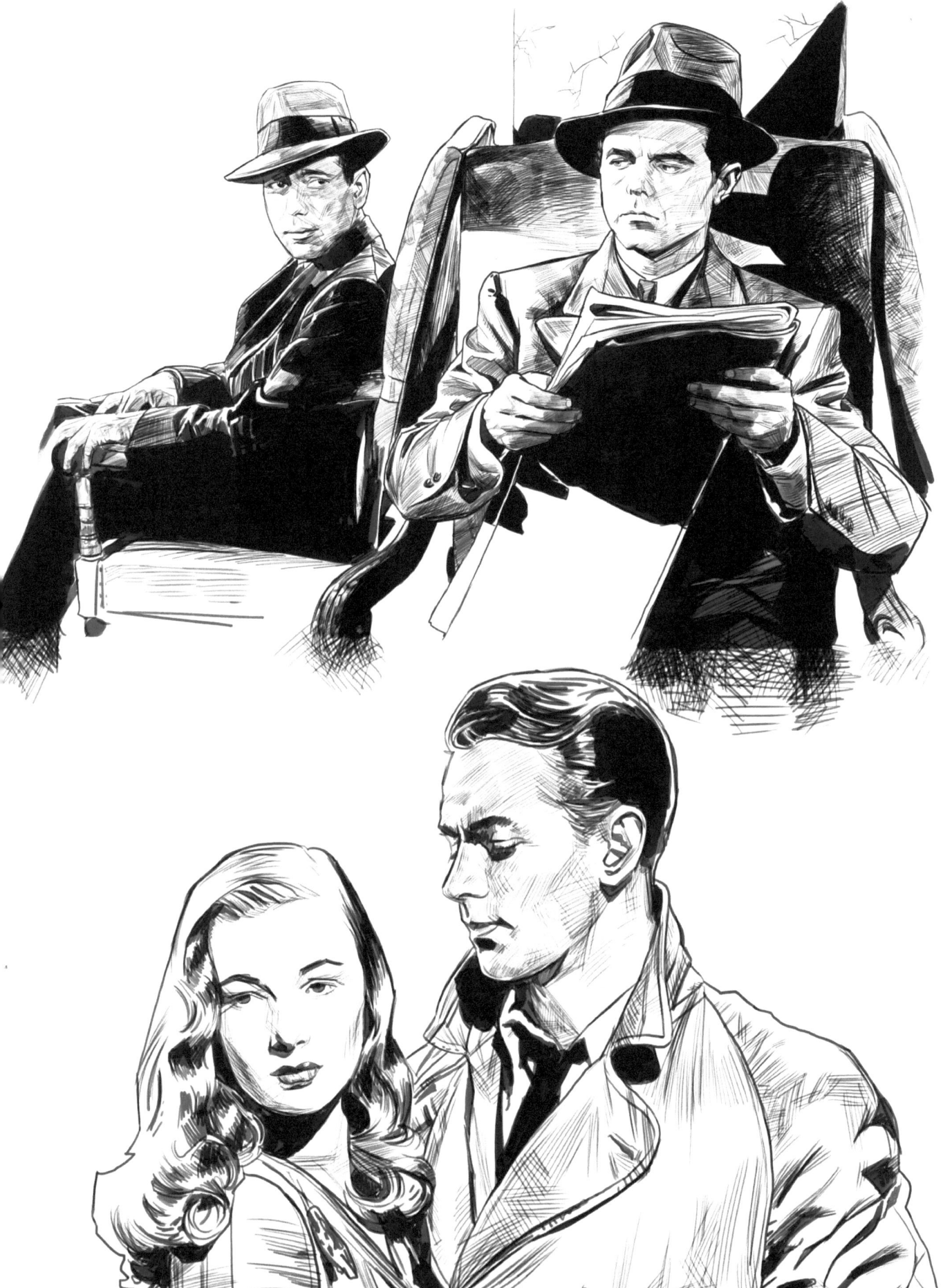

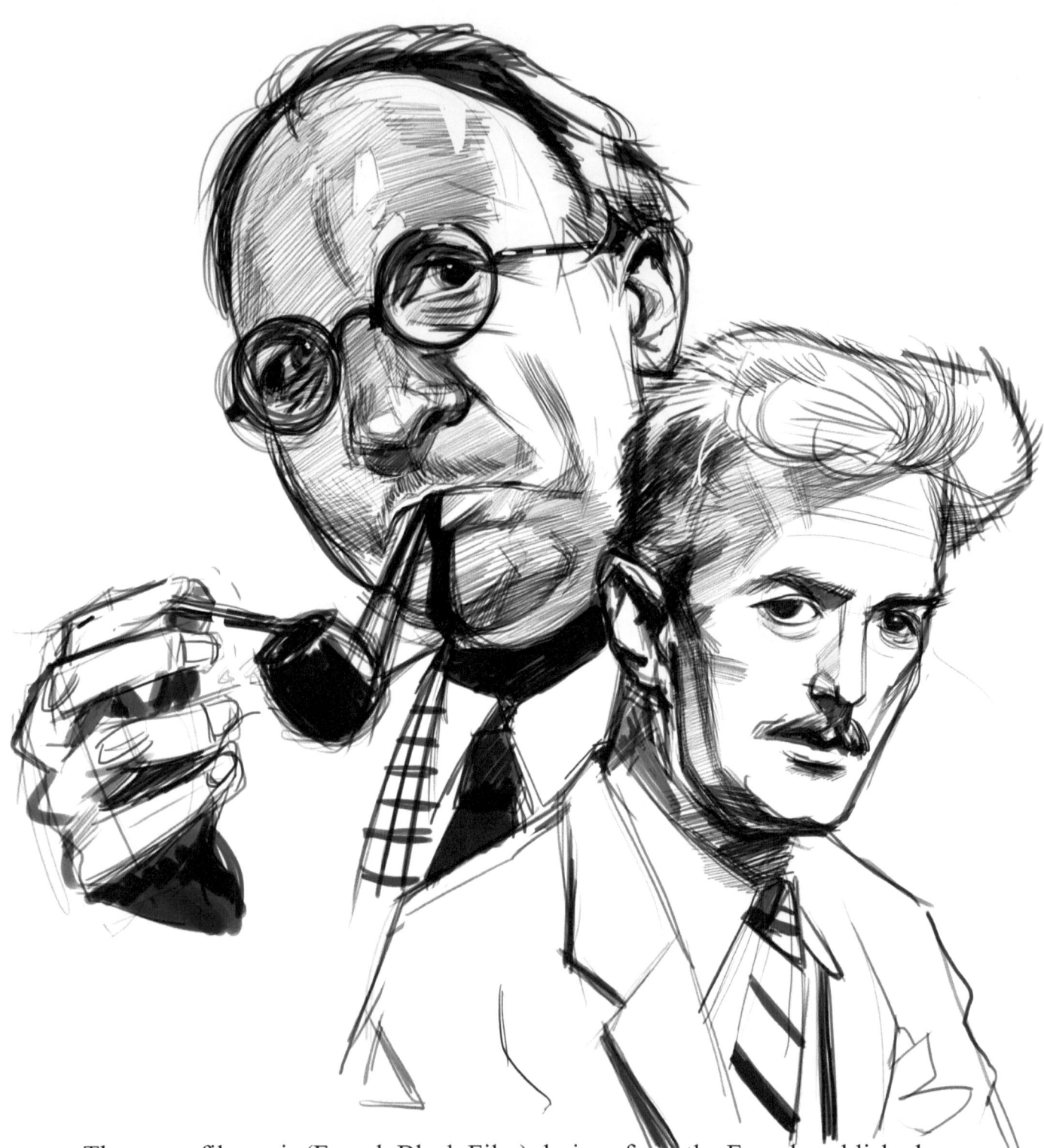

The name film noir (French Black Film) derives from the French-published detective novels (Serie Noire—The Black Series), which include such authors as Raymond Chandler and Dashiell Hammett. French movie critics apply the modified term film noir to a group of dark and cynical American crime movies which emerge in the first half of the 1940s.

The pronounced negativism of Double Indemnity is accentuated by the theme of moral corruption and adultery—vices never before presented on the American screen with such relentless accuracy.

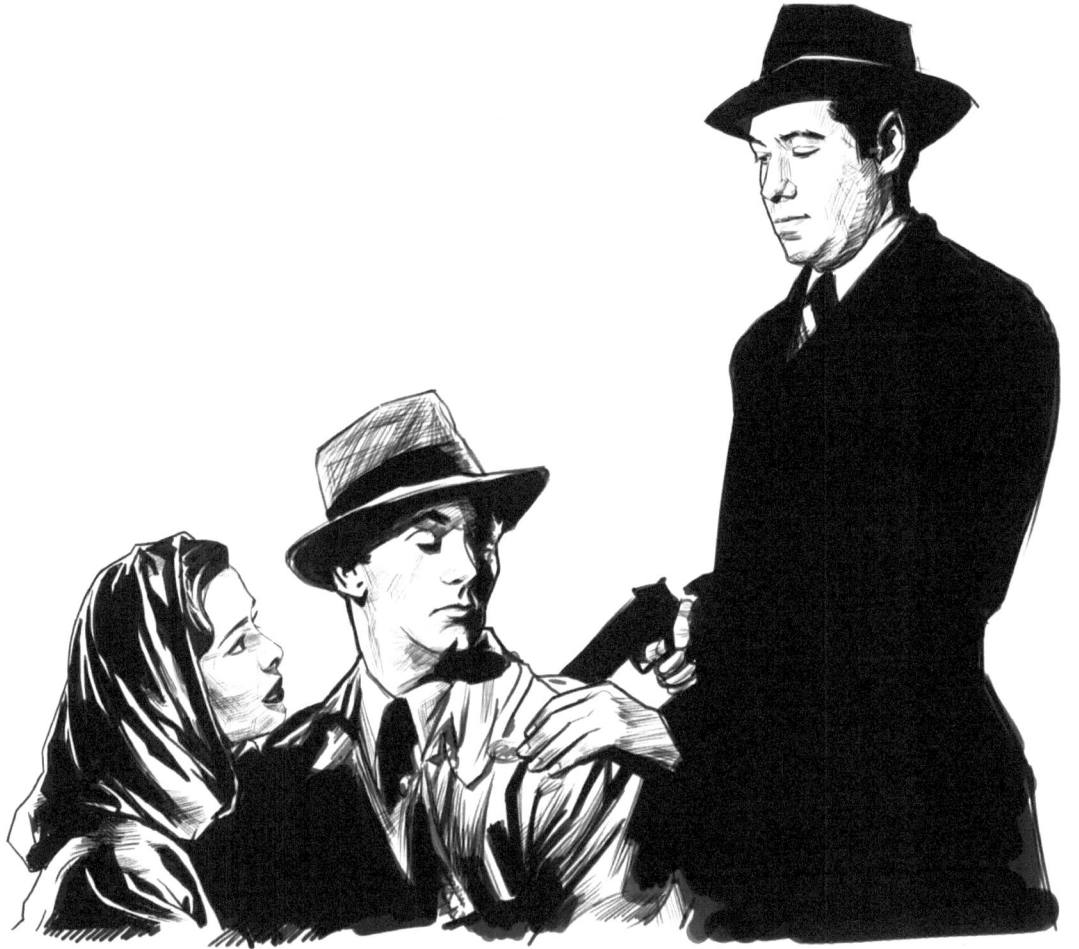

Out of the Past shatters all illusions of human loyalty and trust, throwing its hapless hero into the abyss of multiple betrayal.

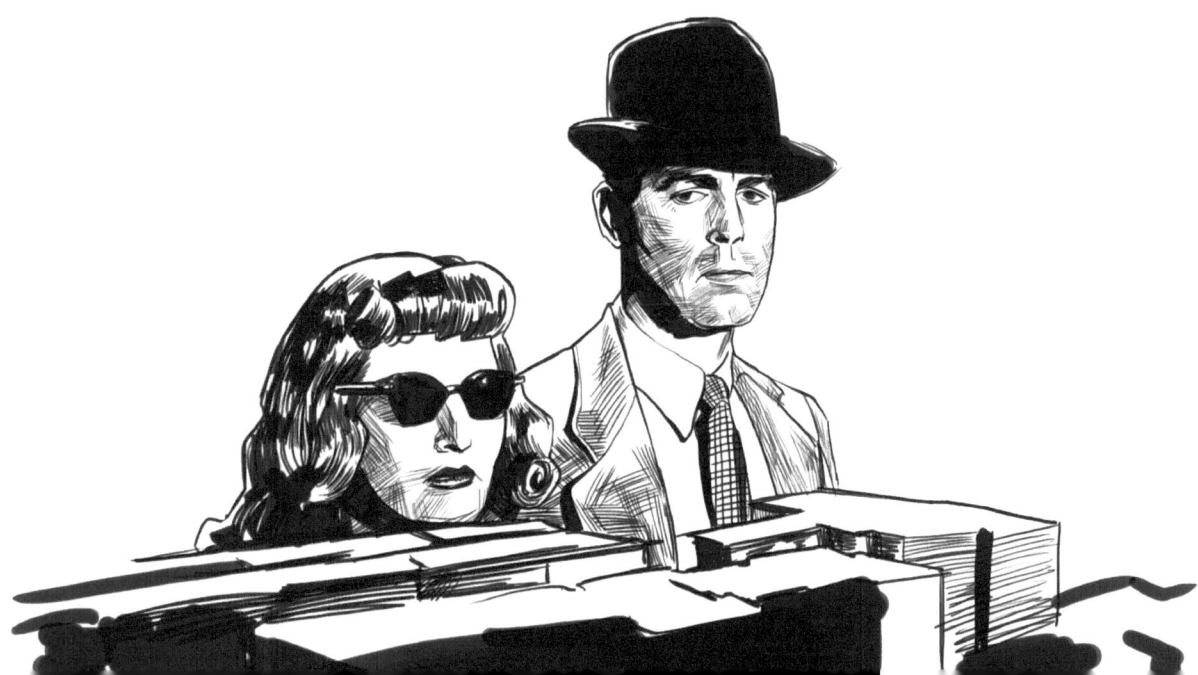

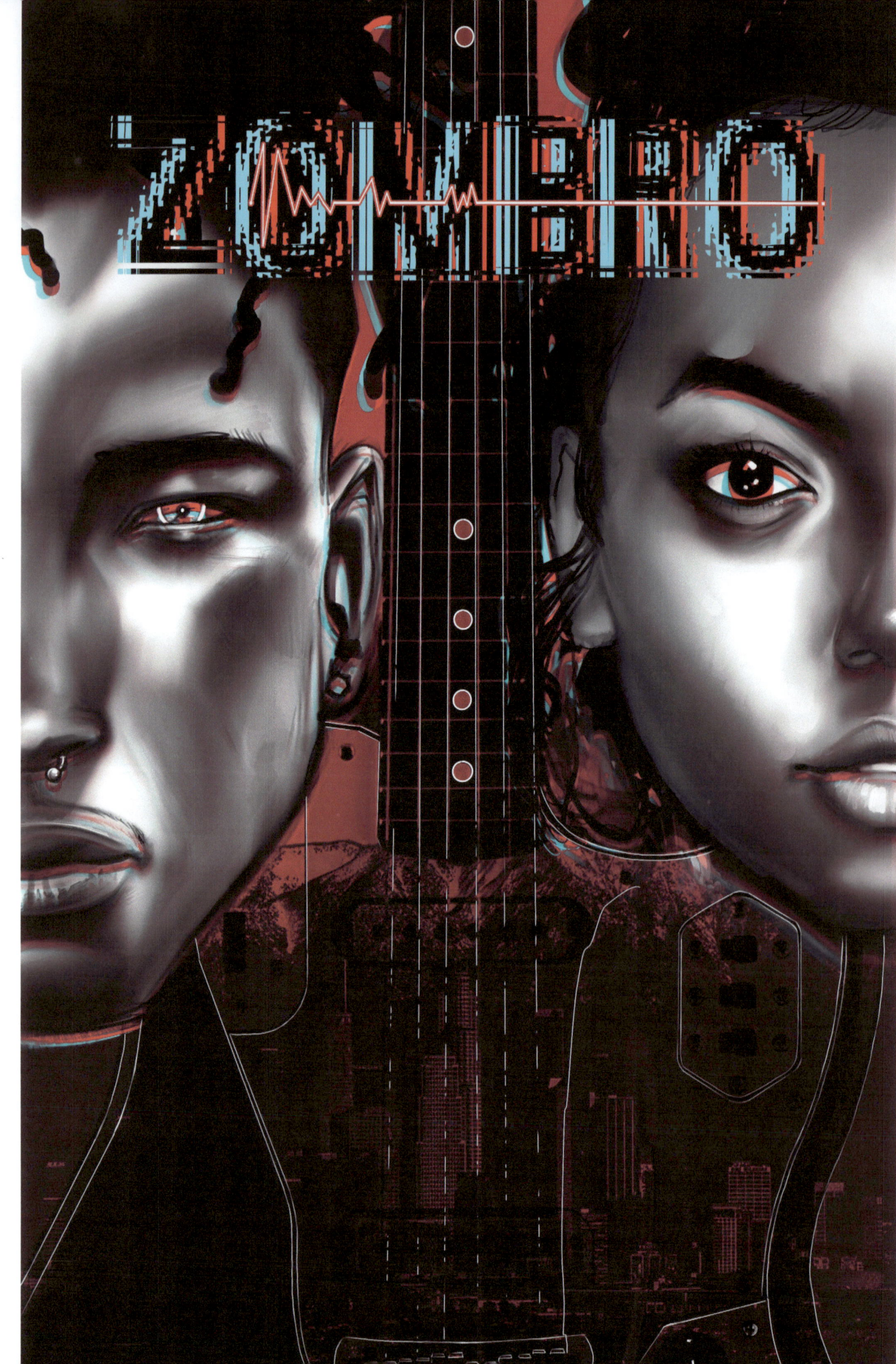

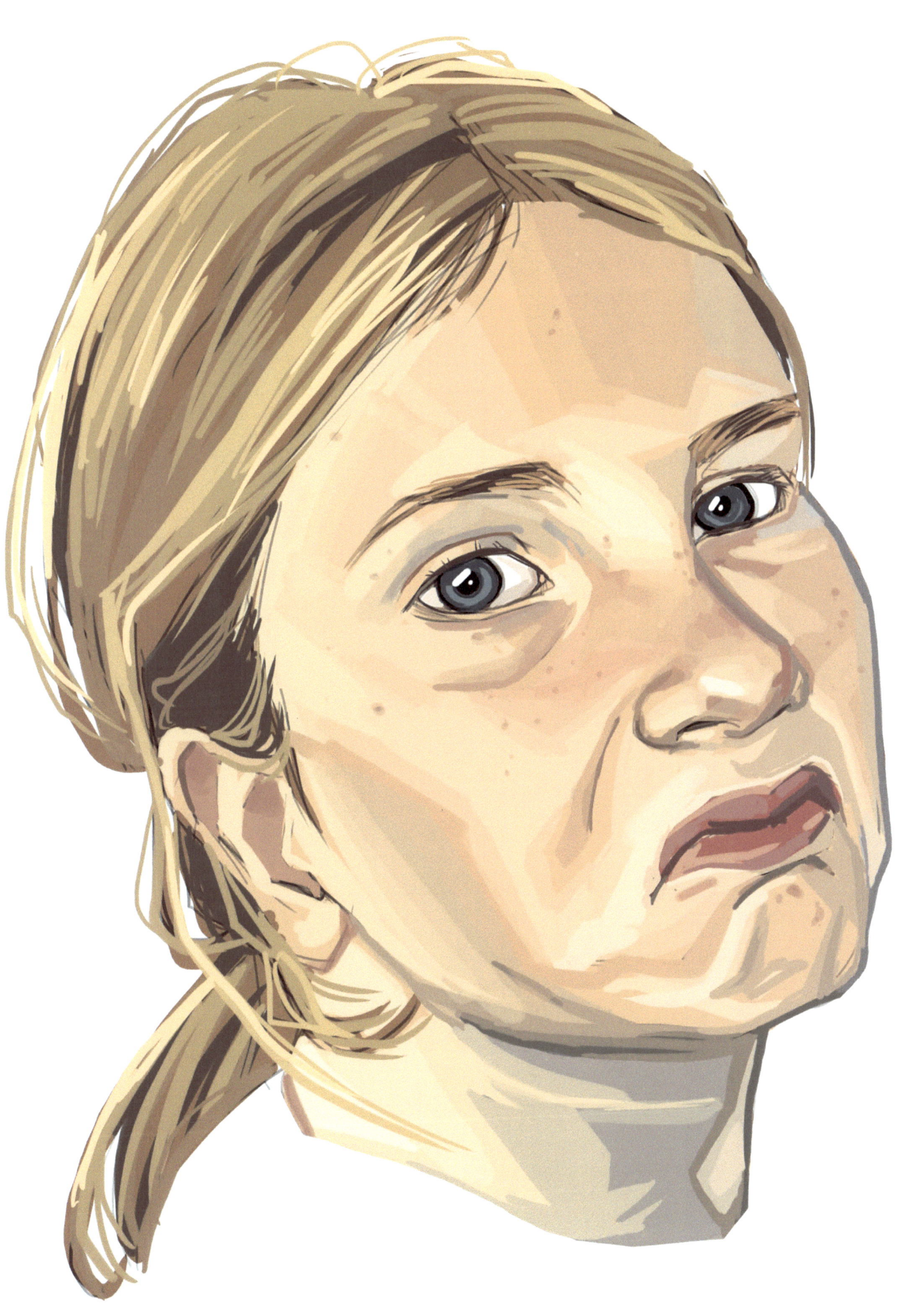

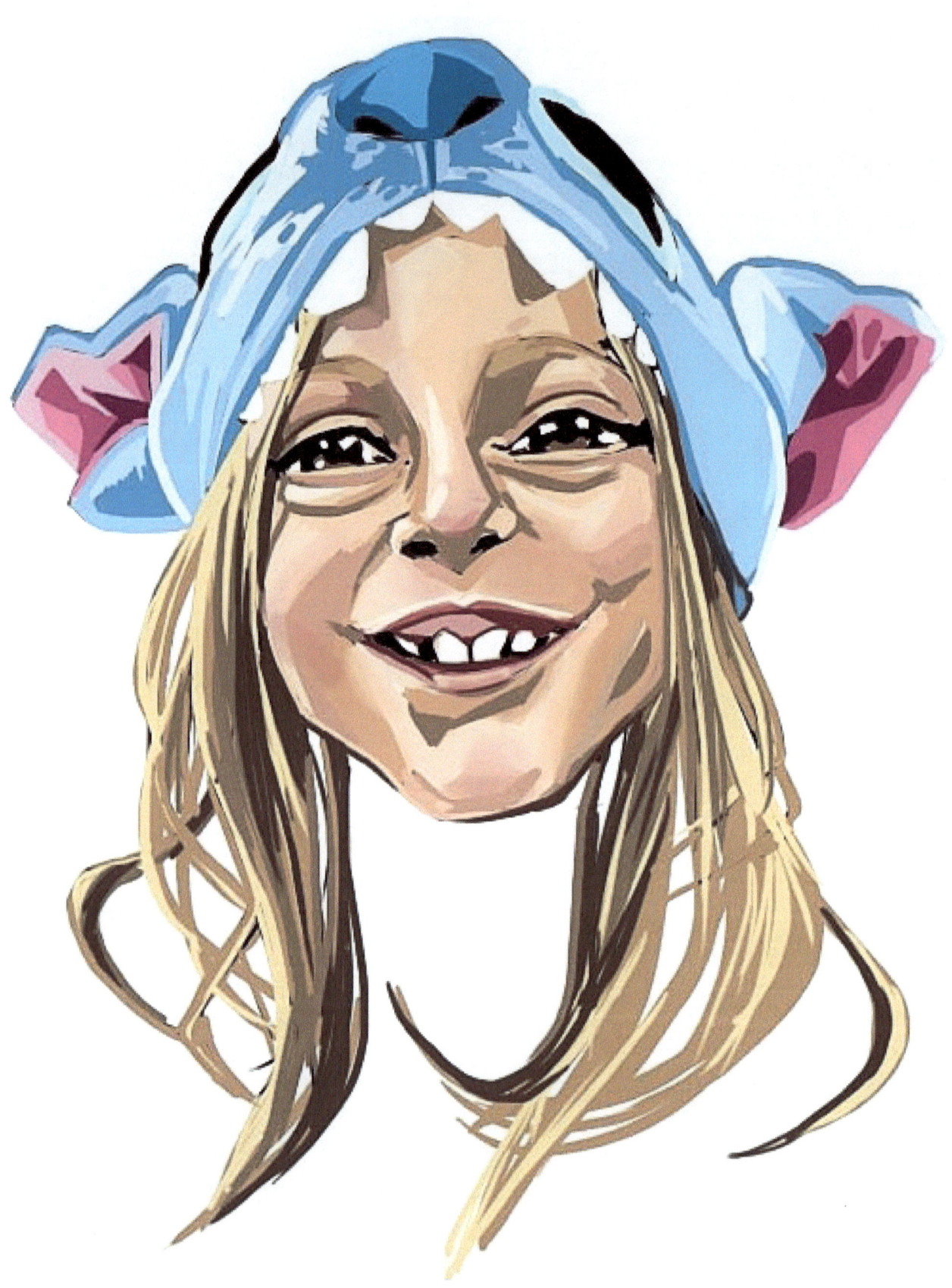

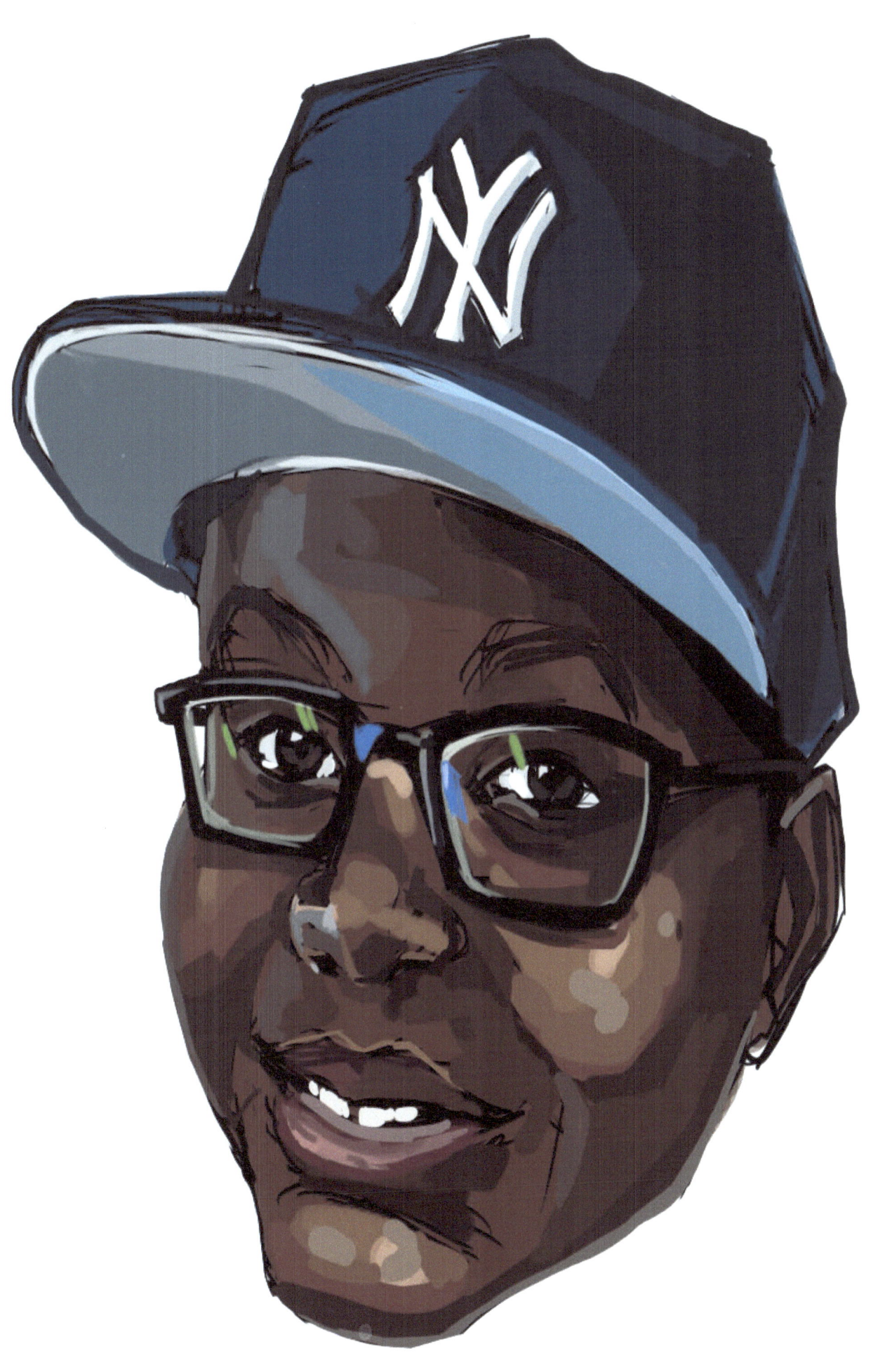

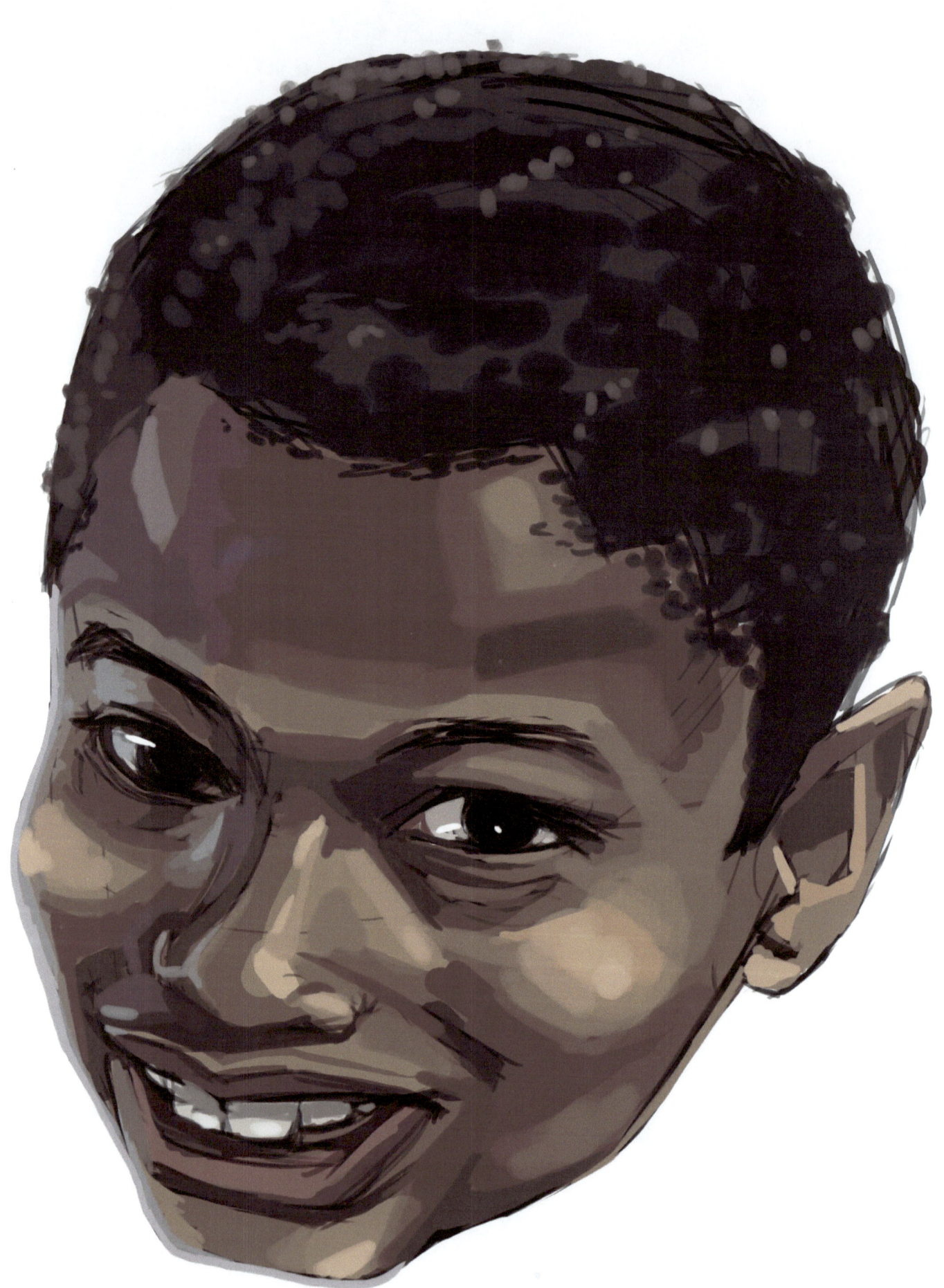

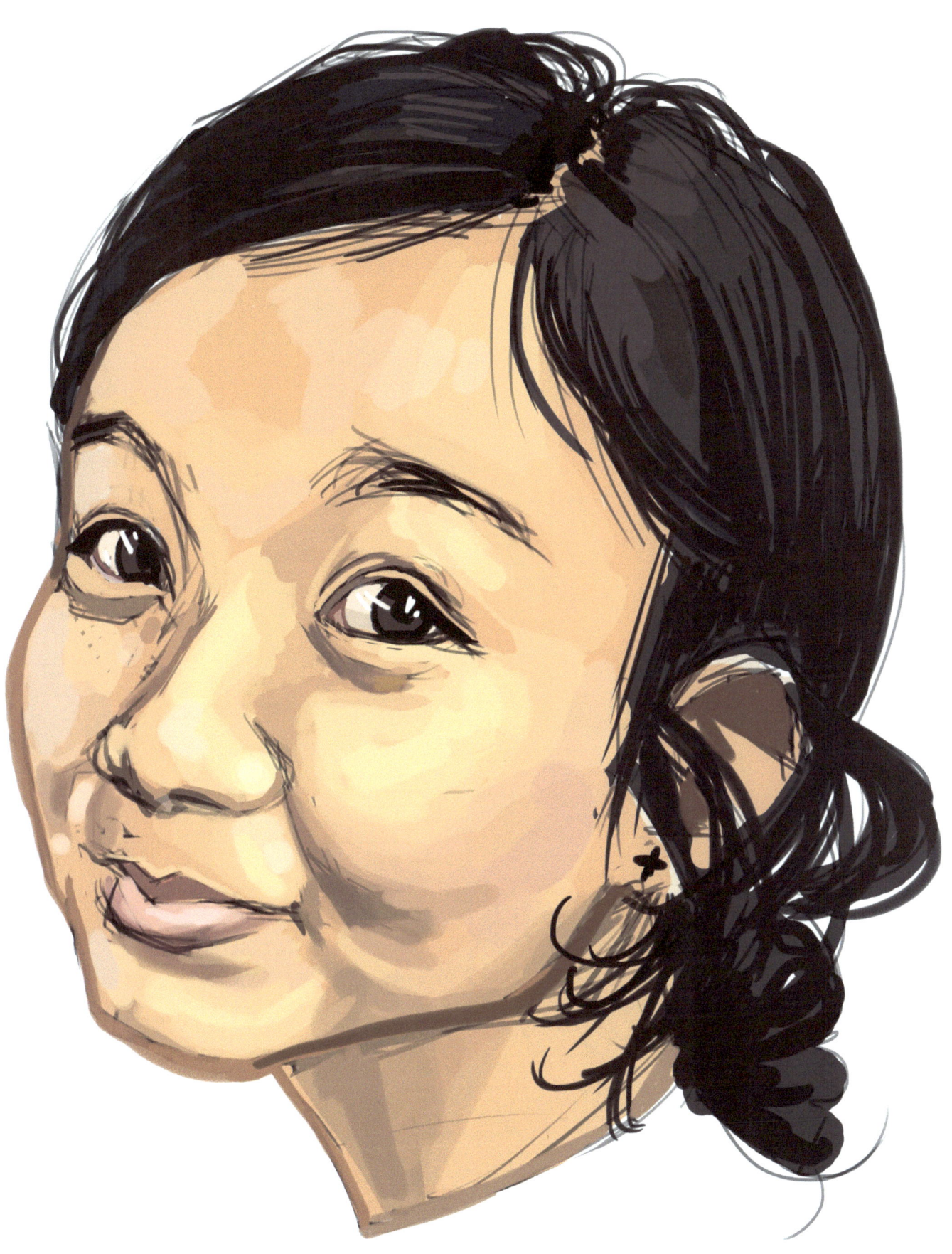

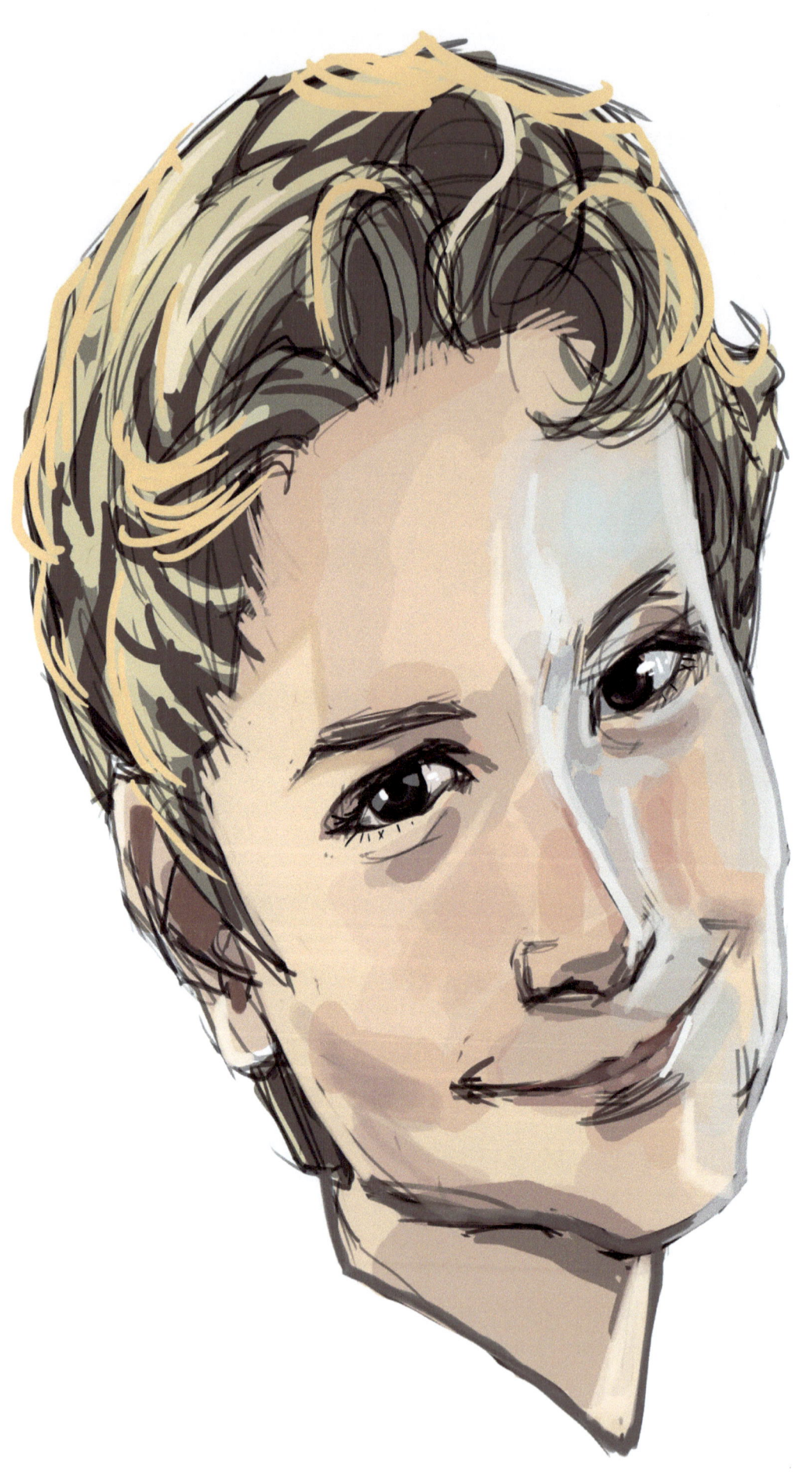

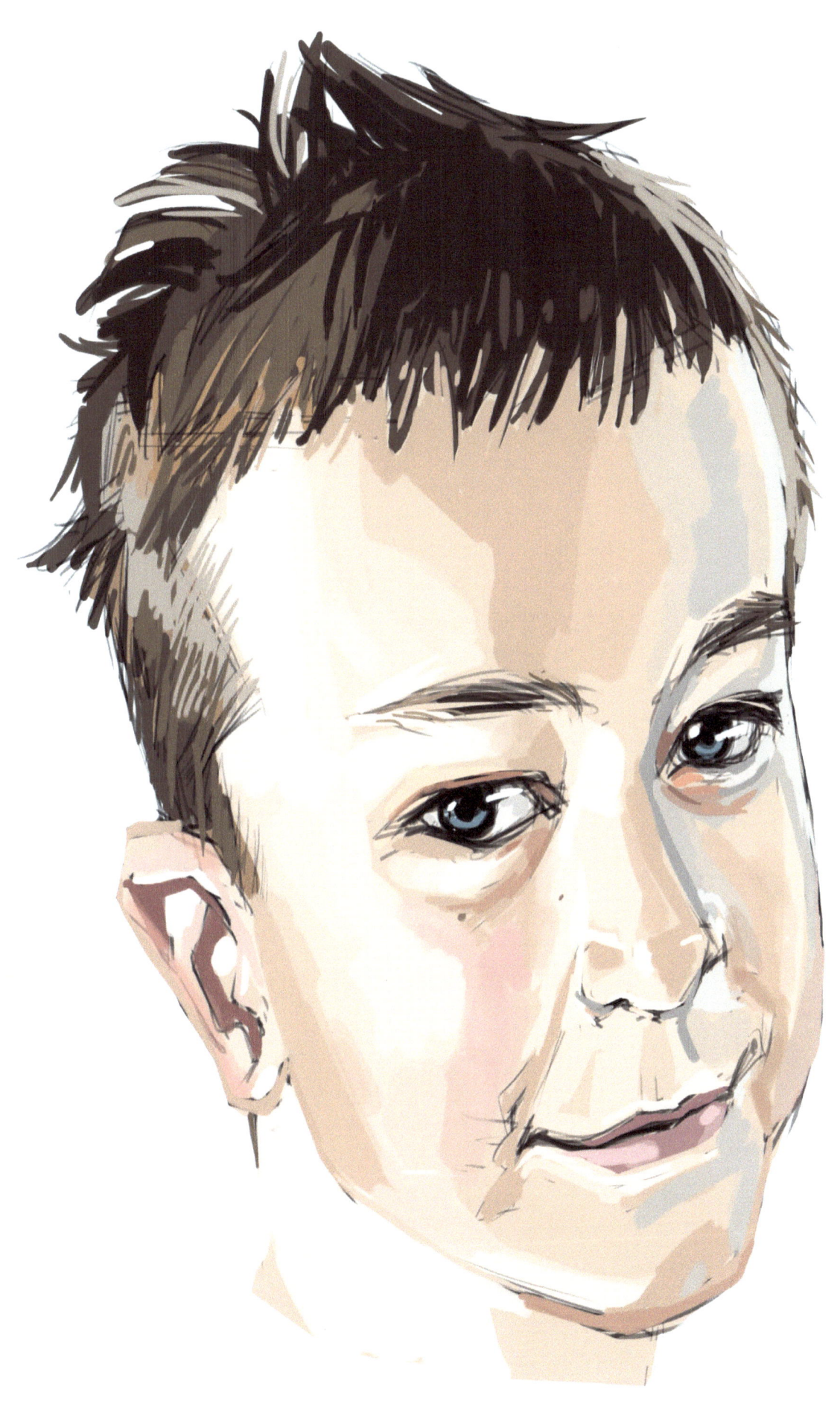

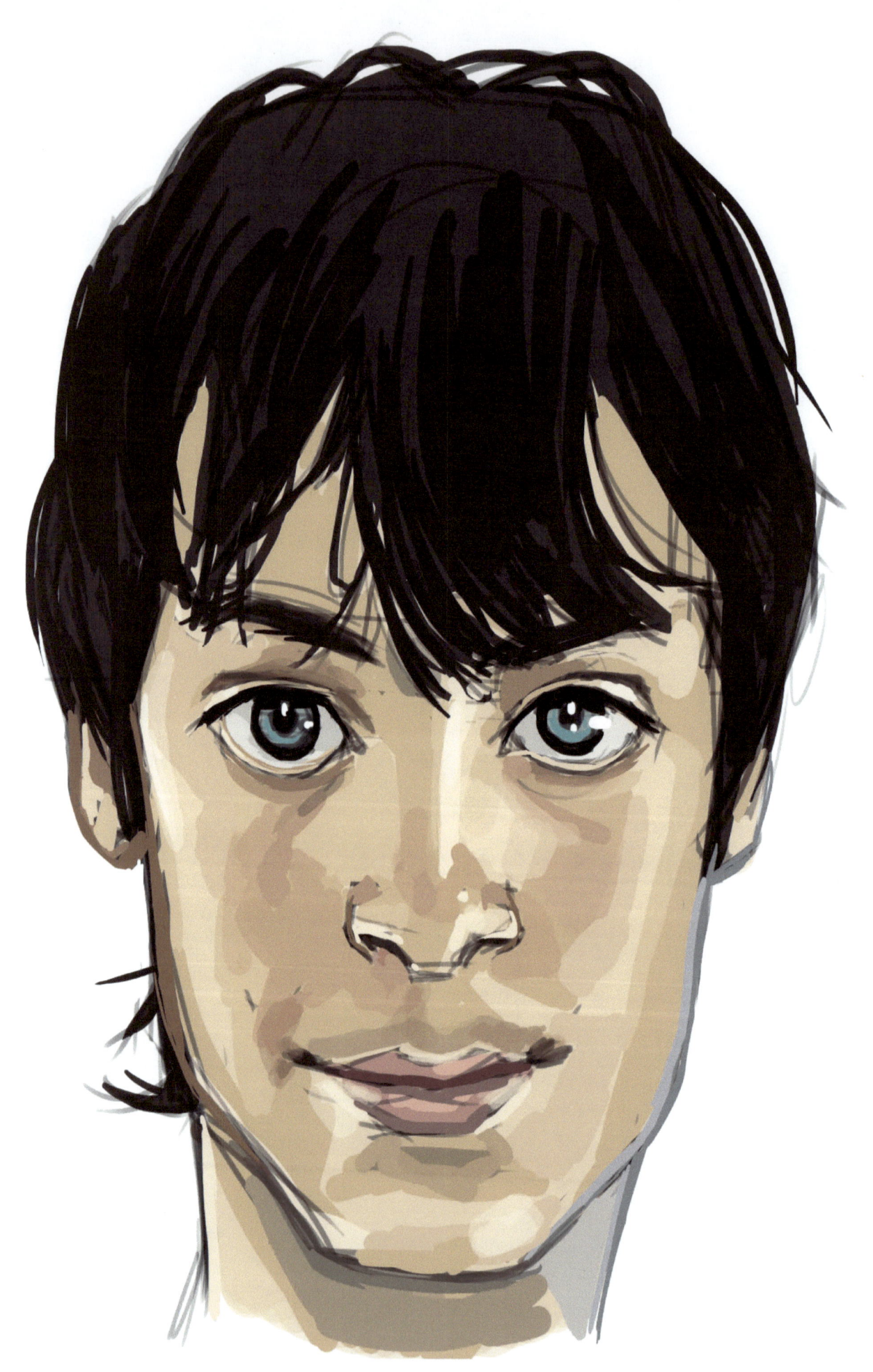

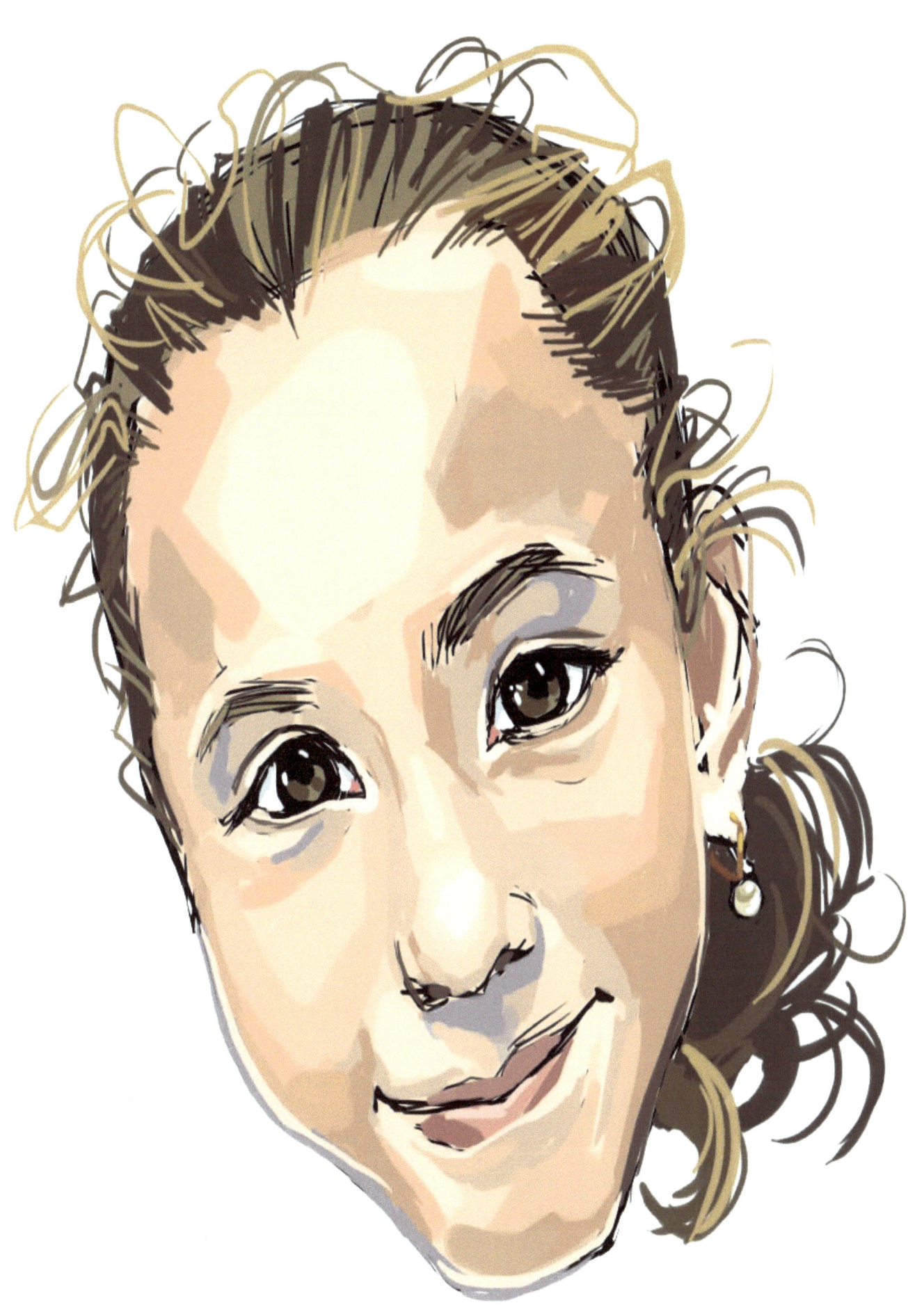

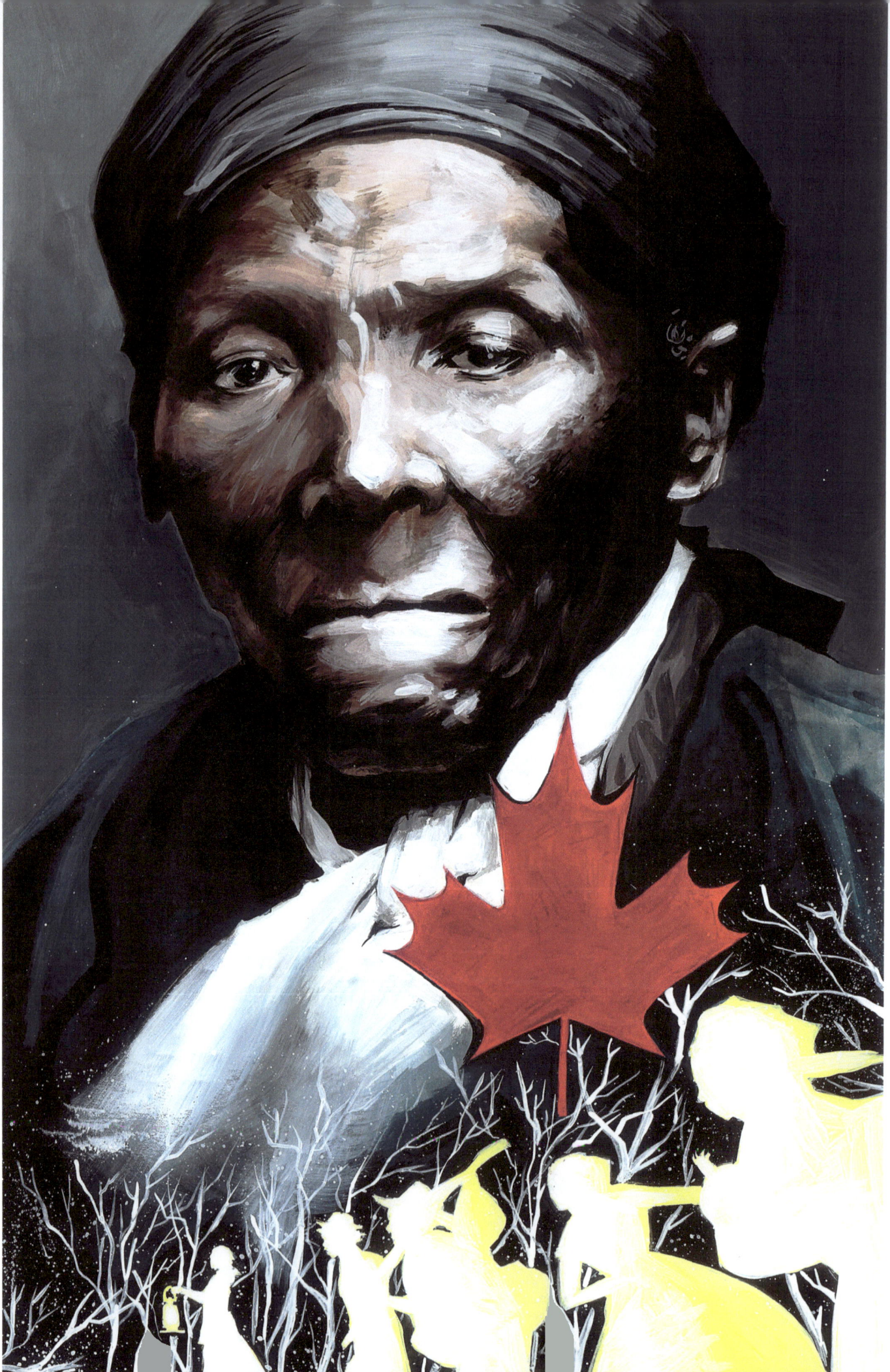

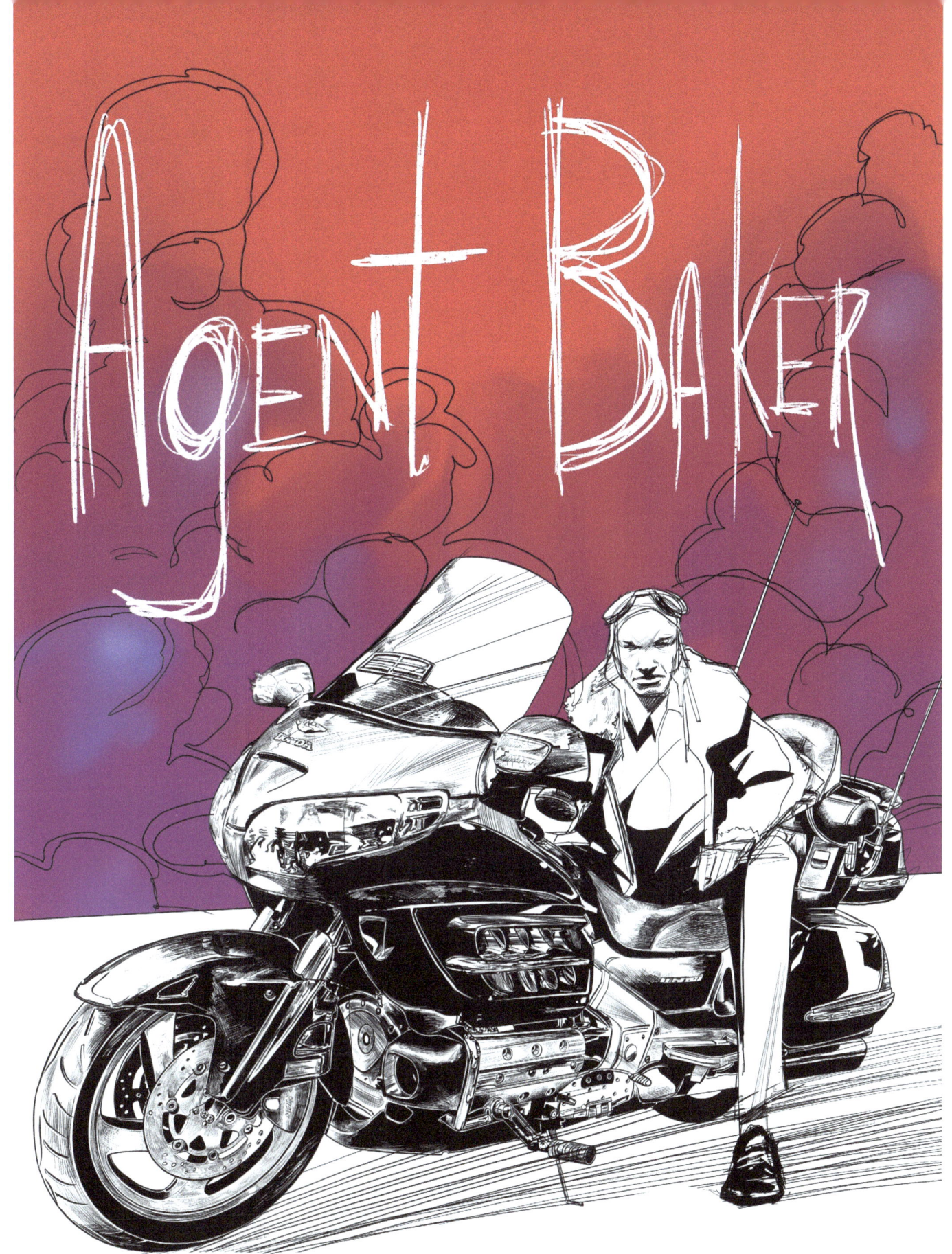

TIDES IN TIME

JESSIE SIFFORD

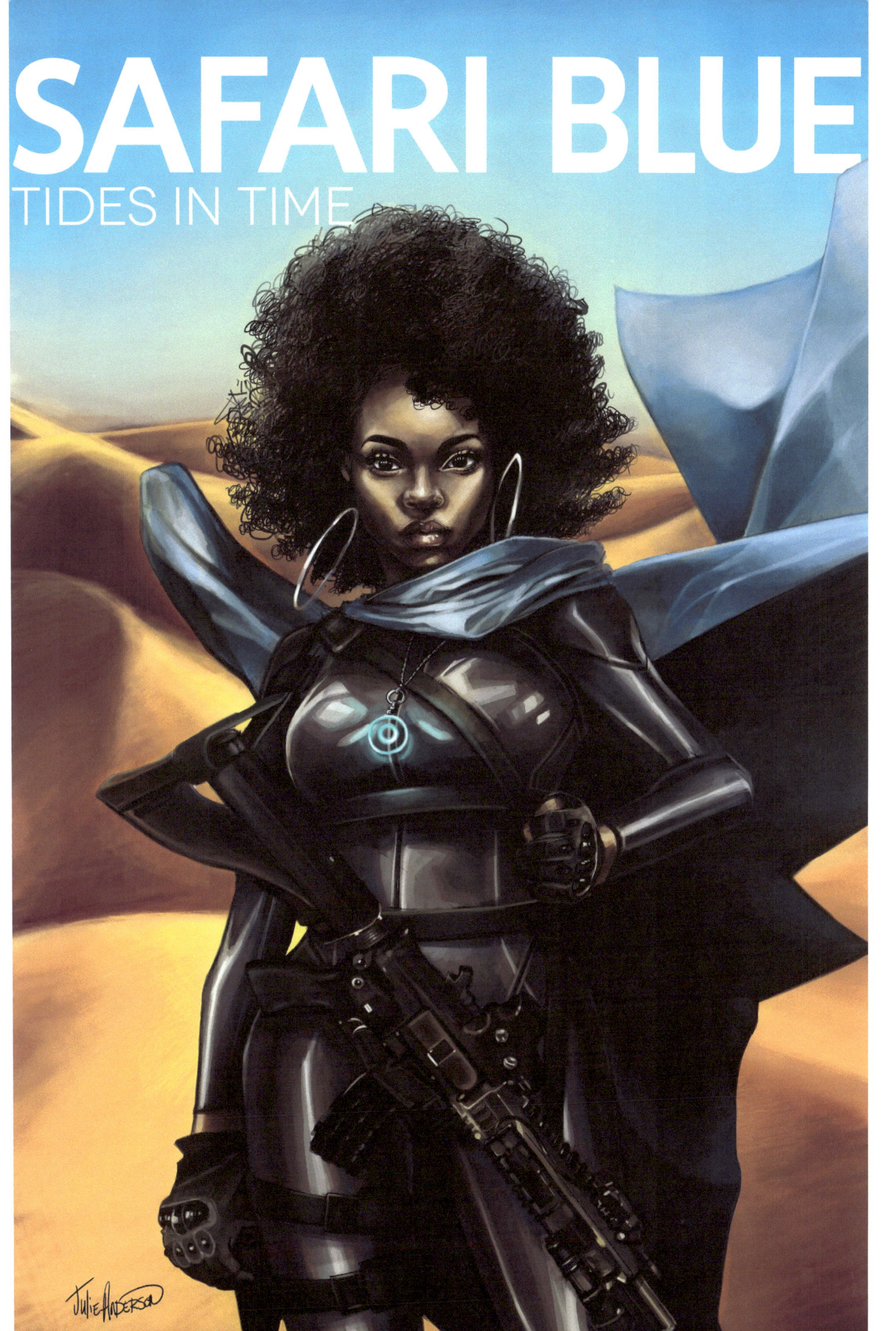

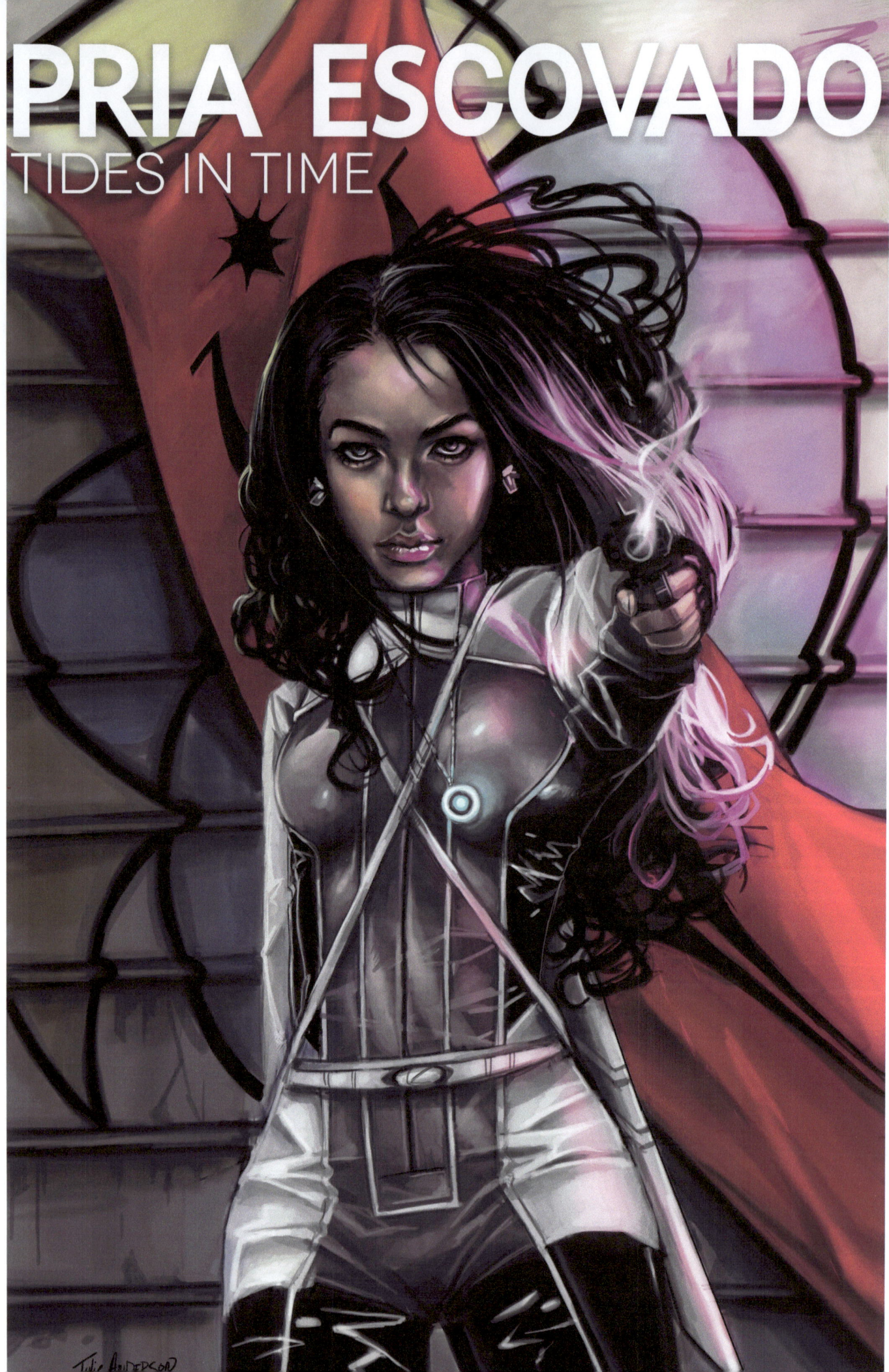

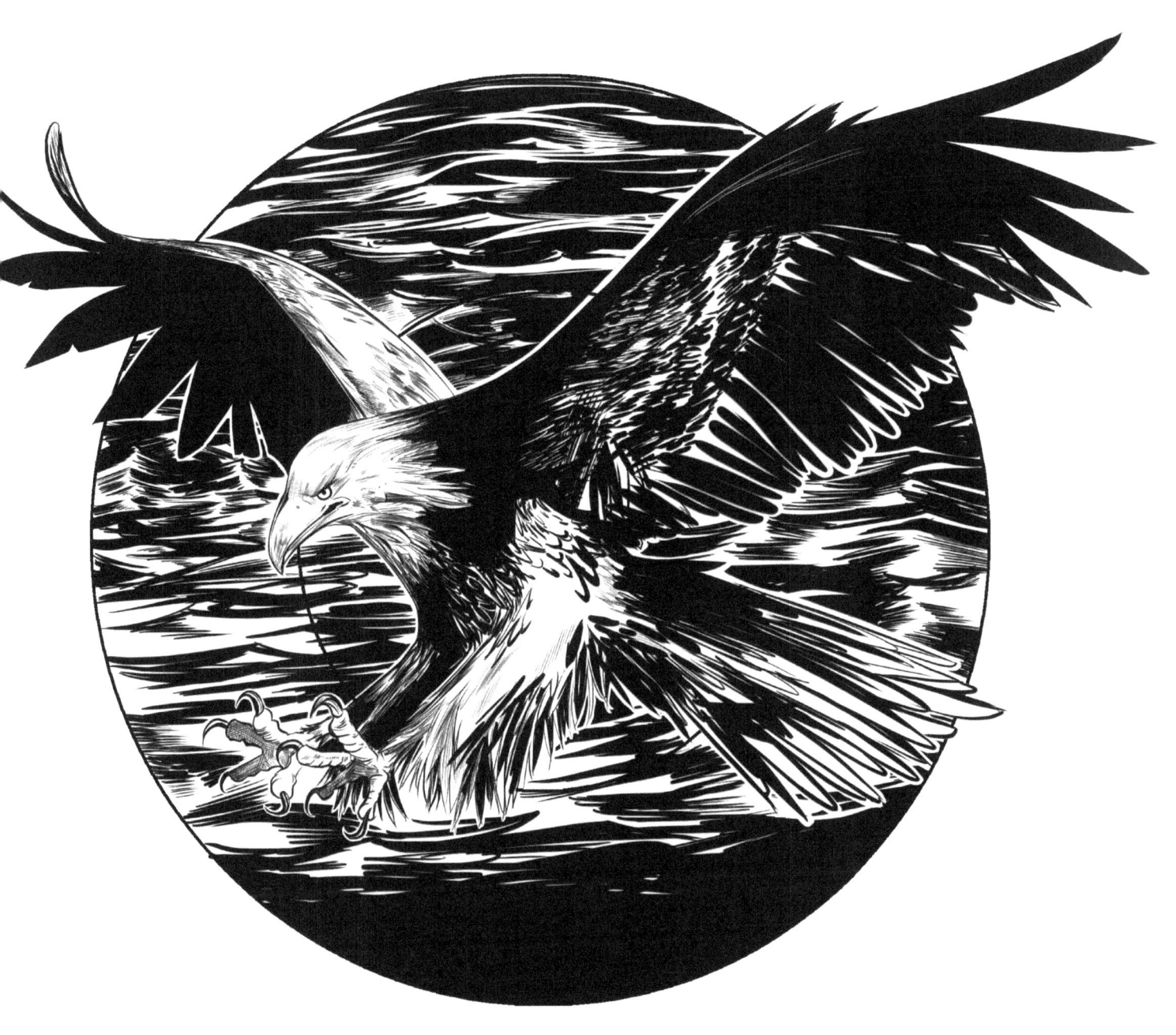

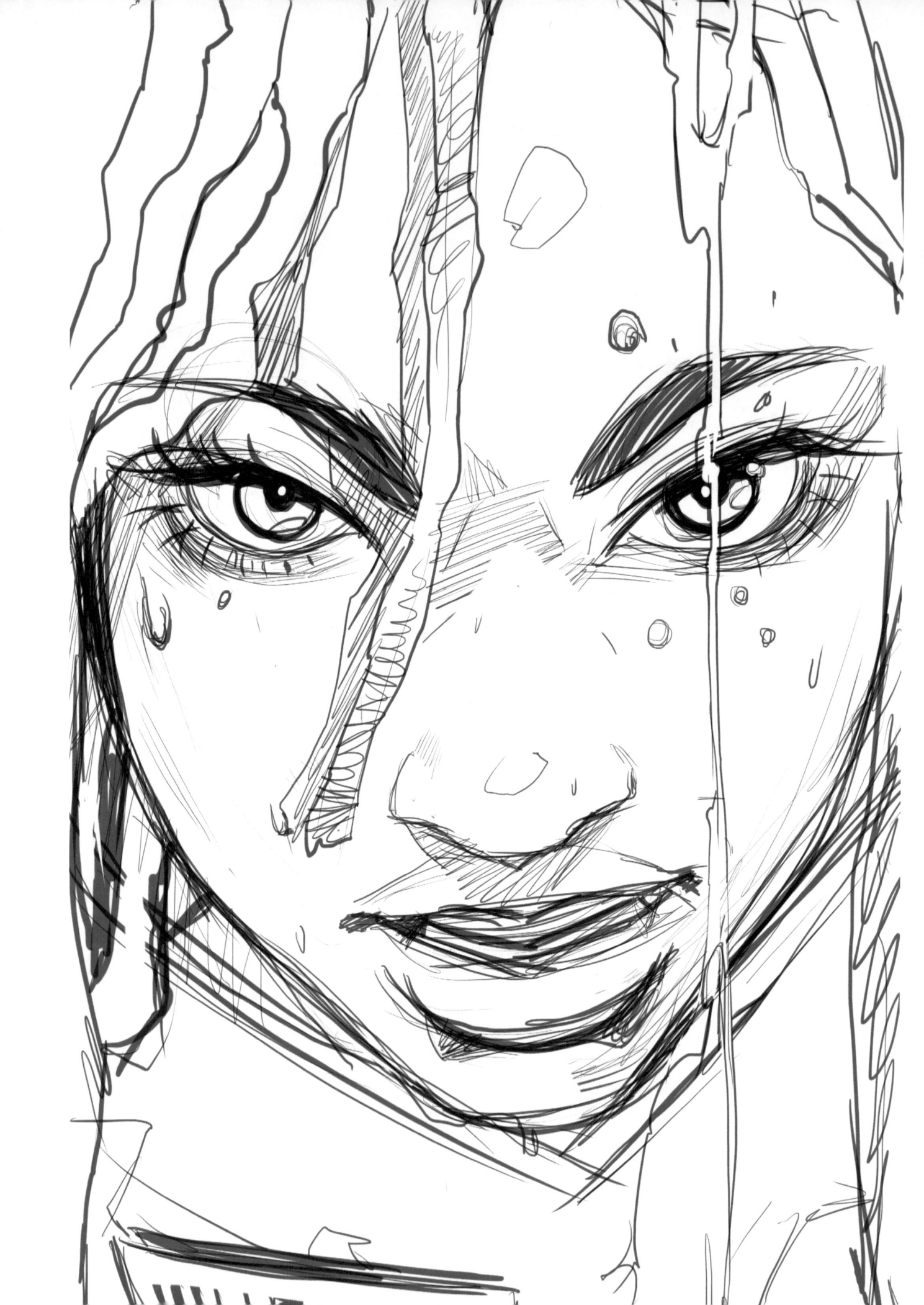

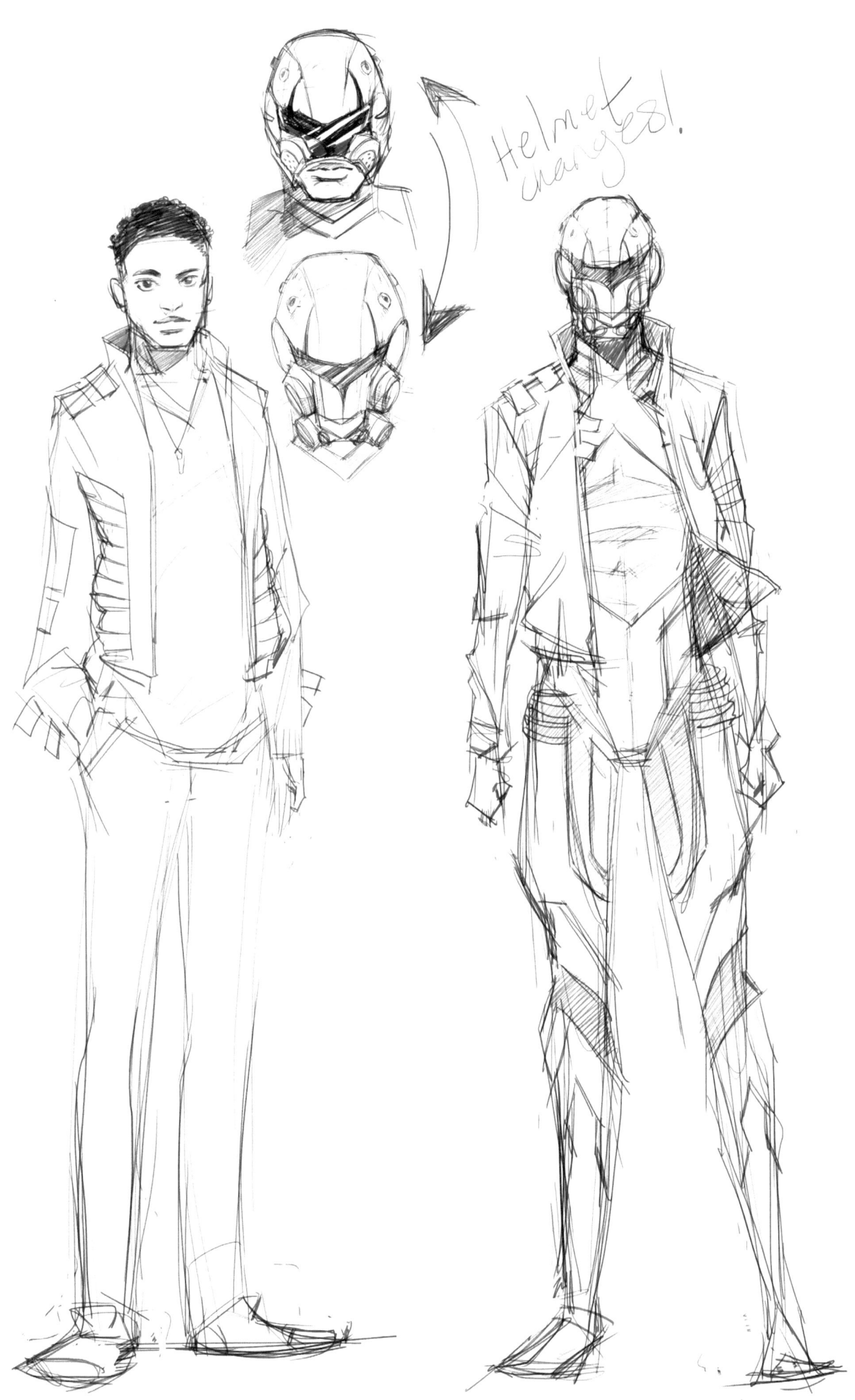

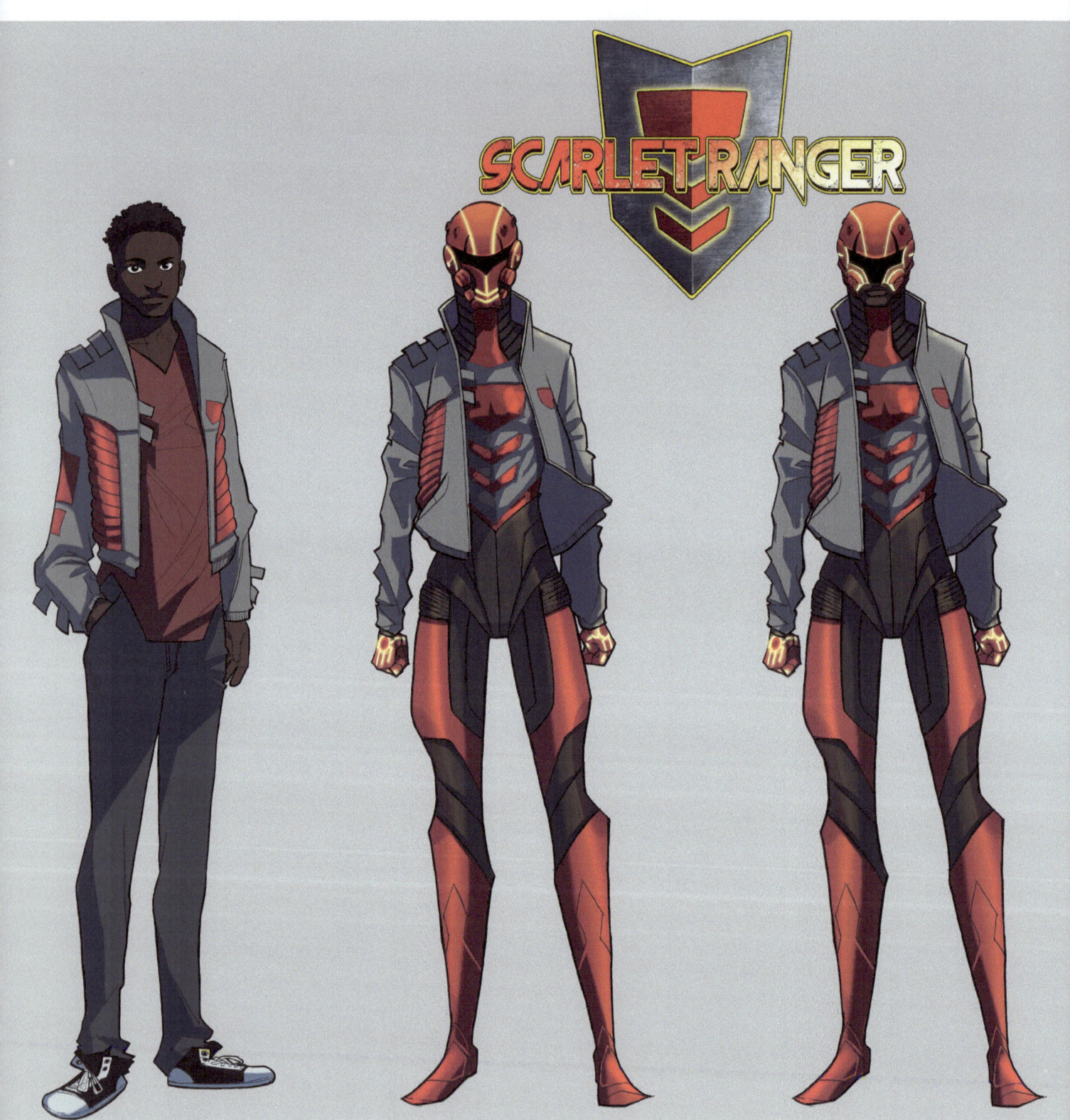

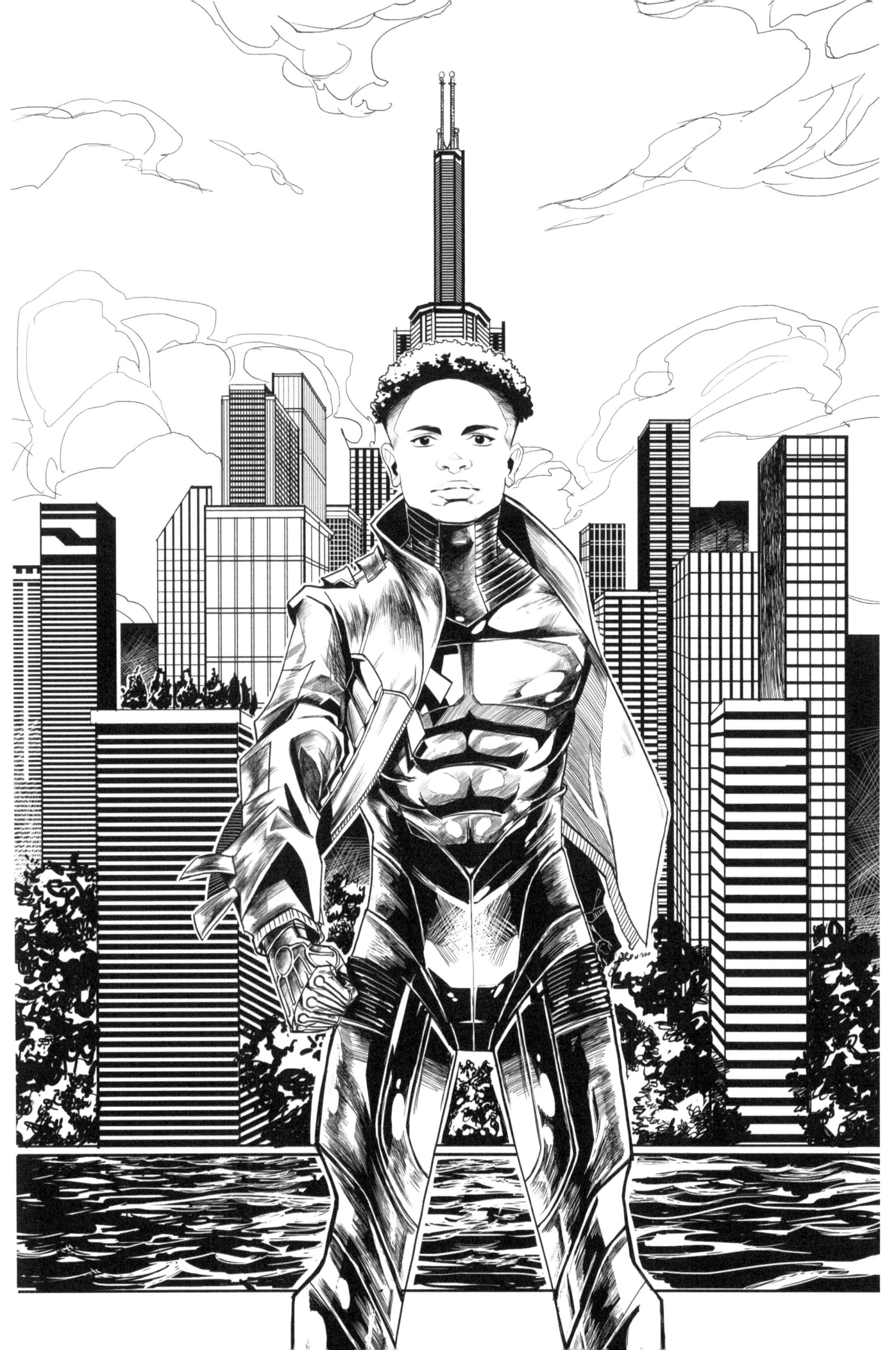

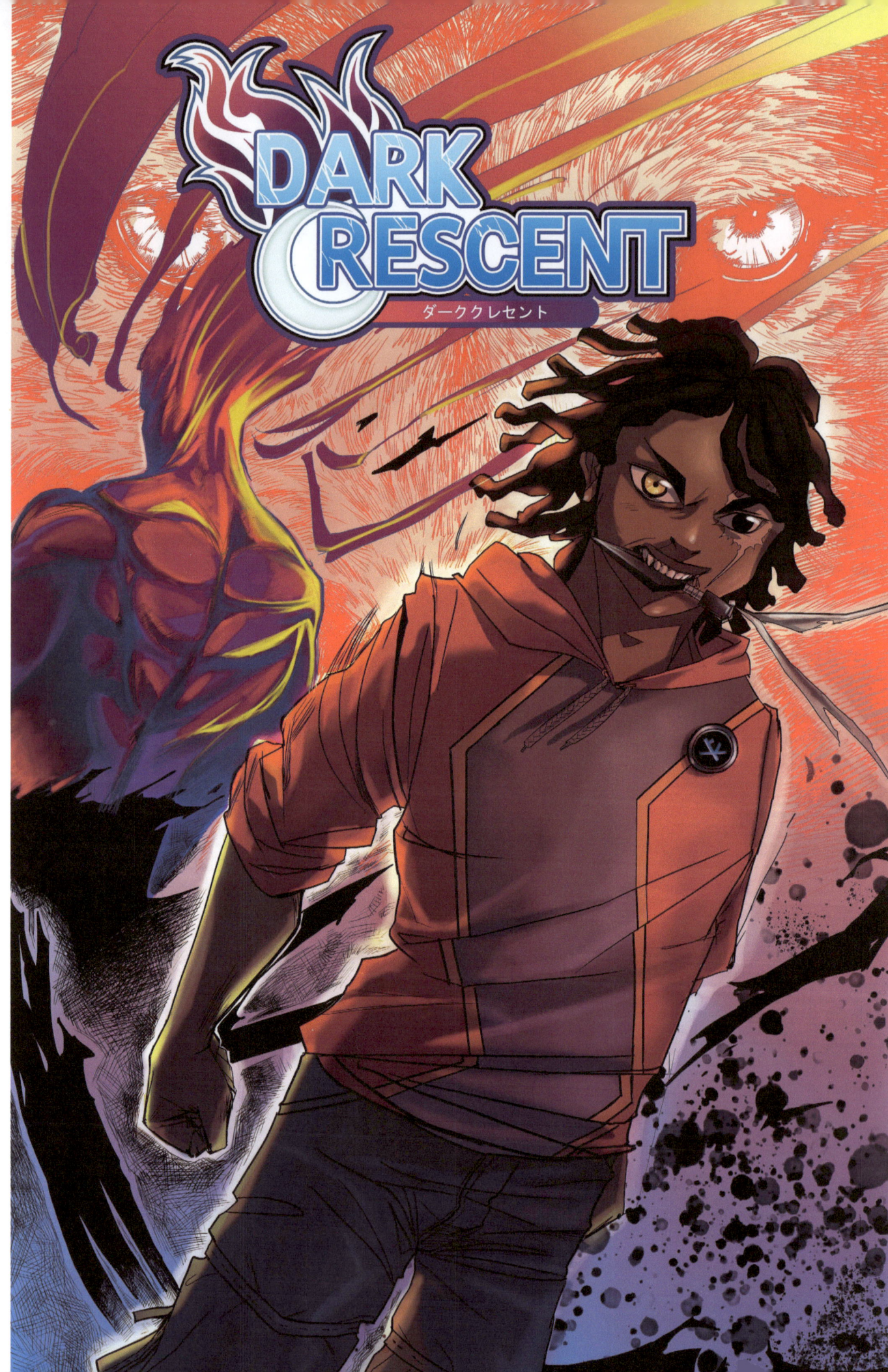

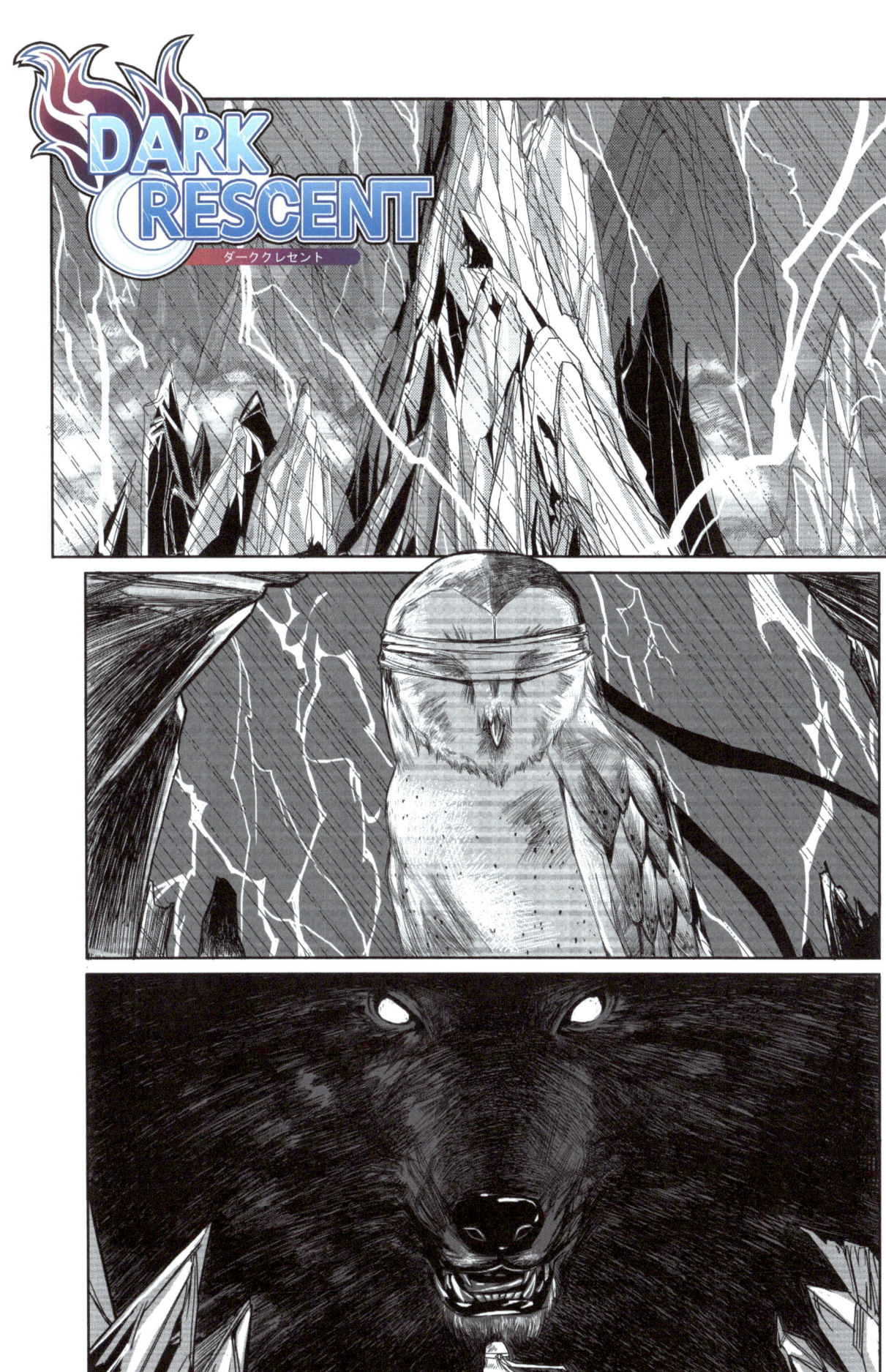

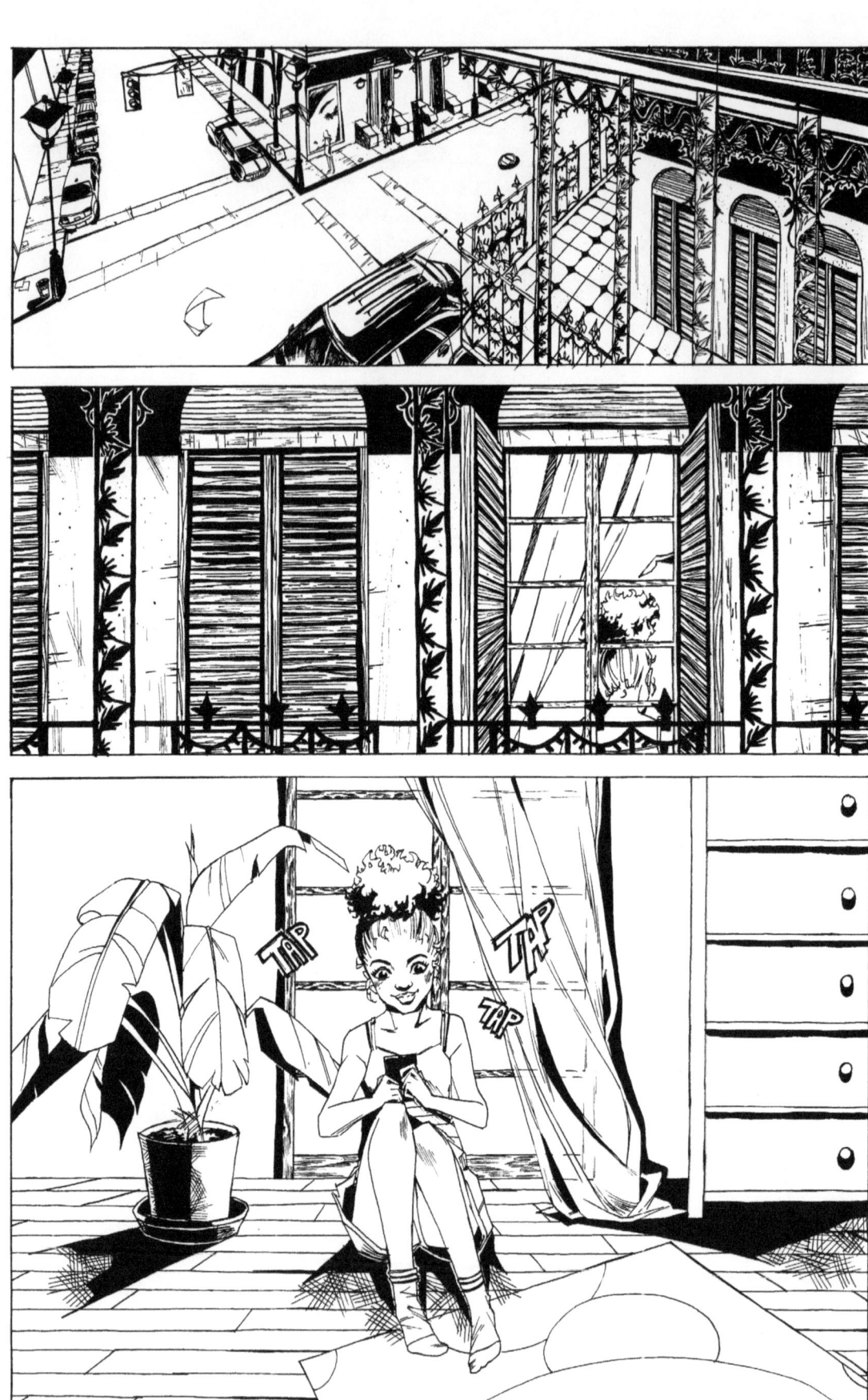

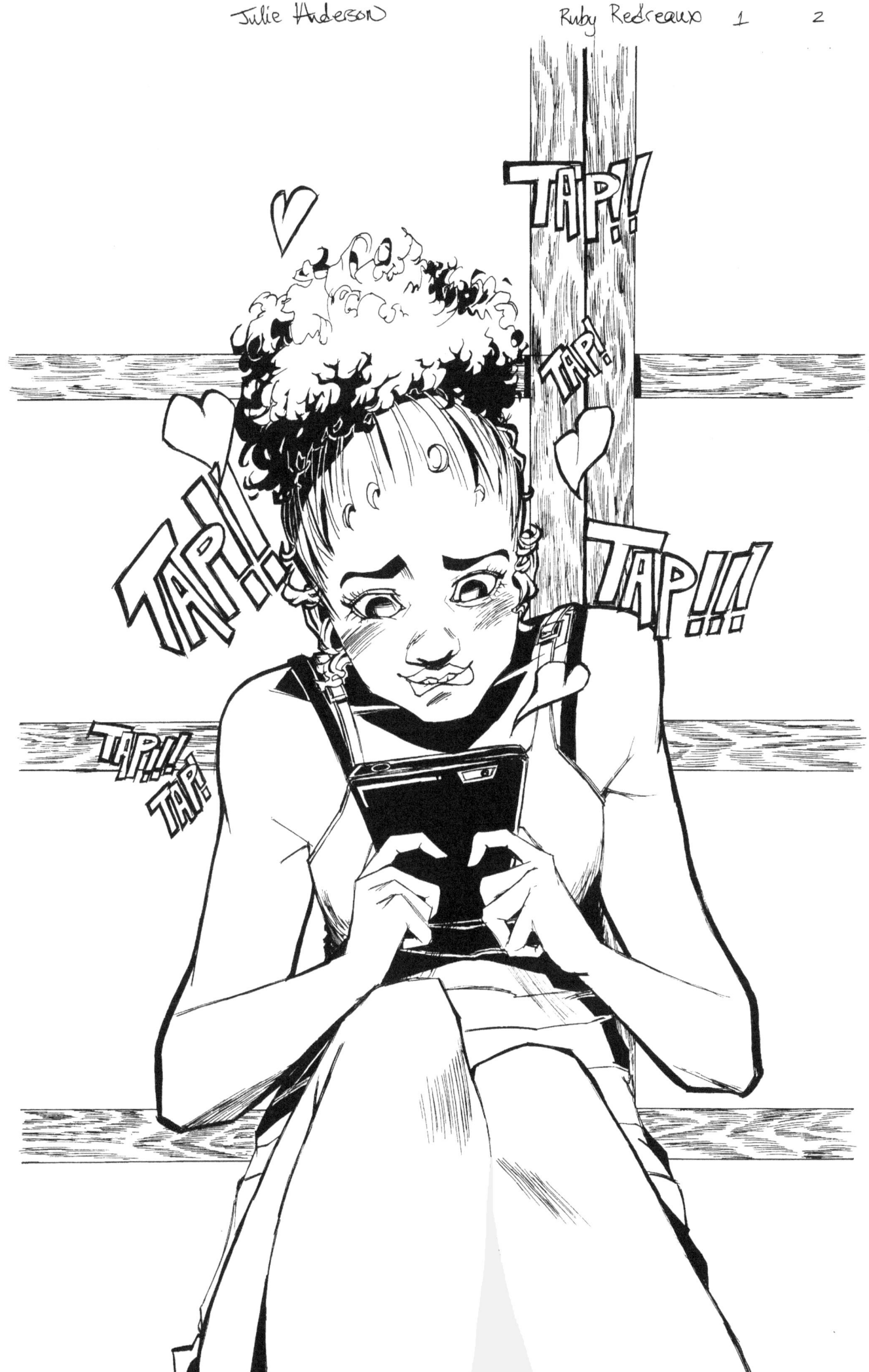

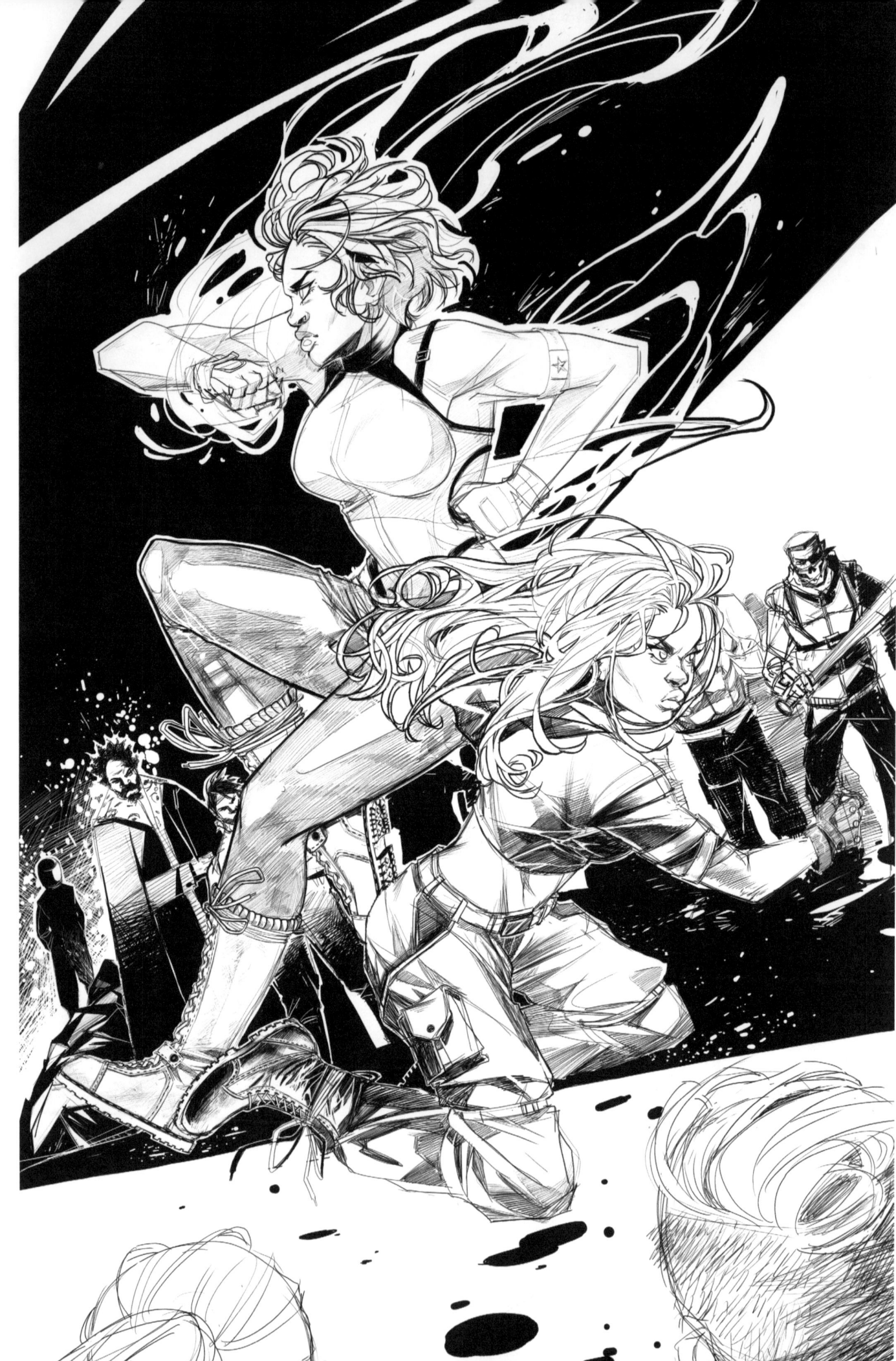

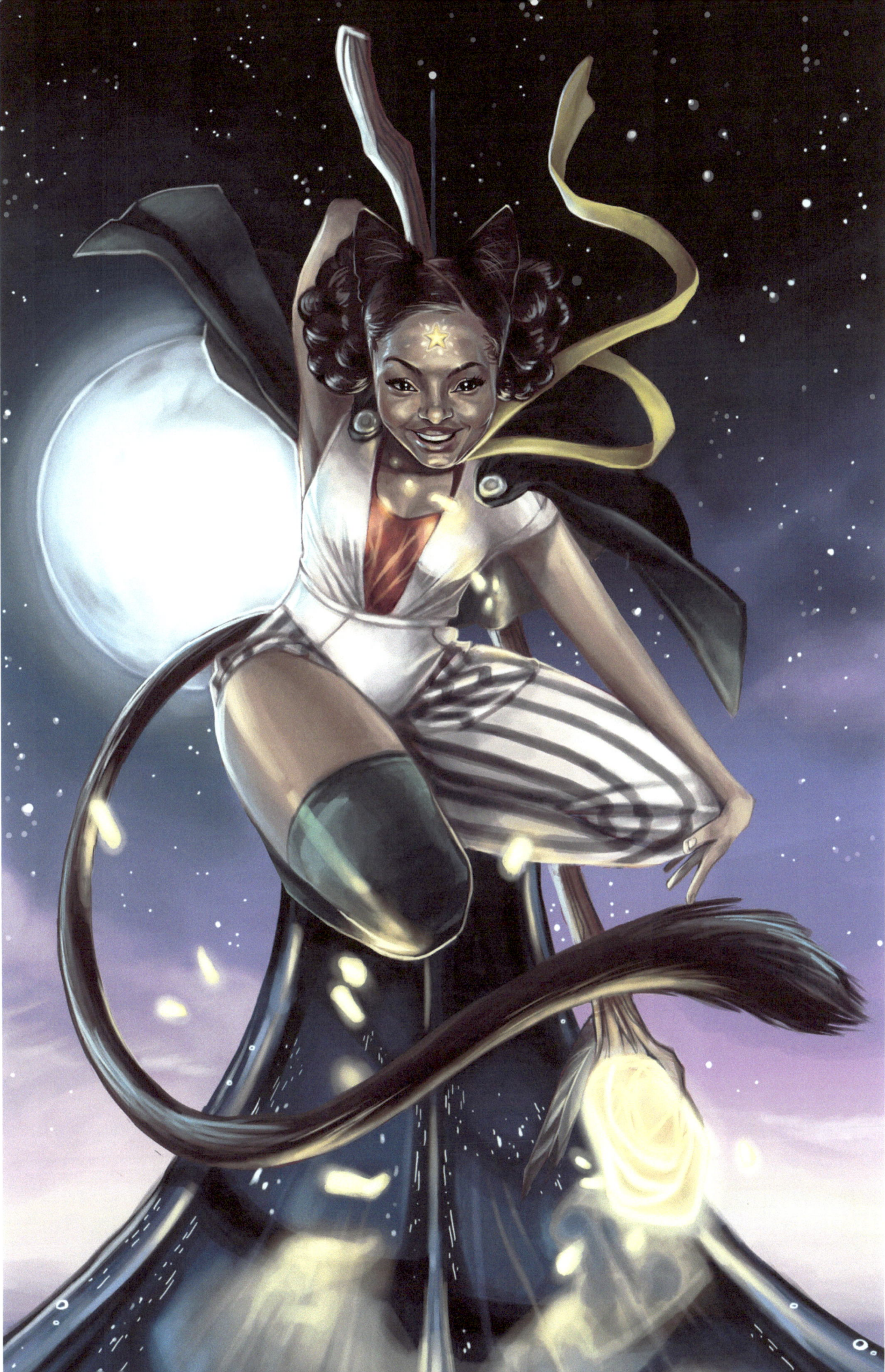

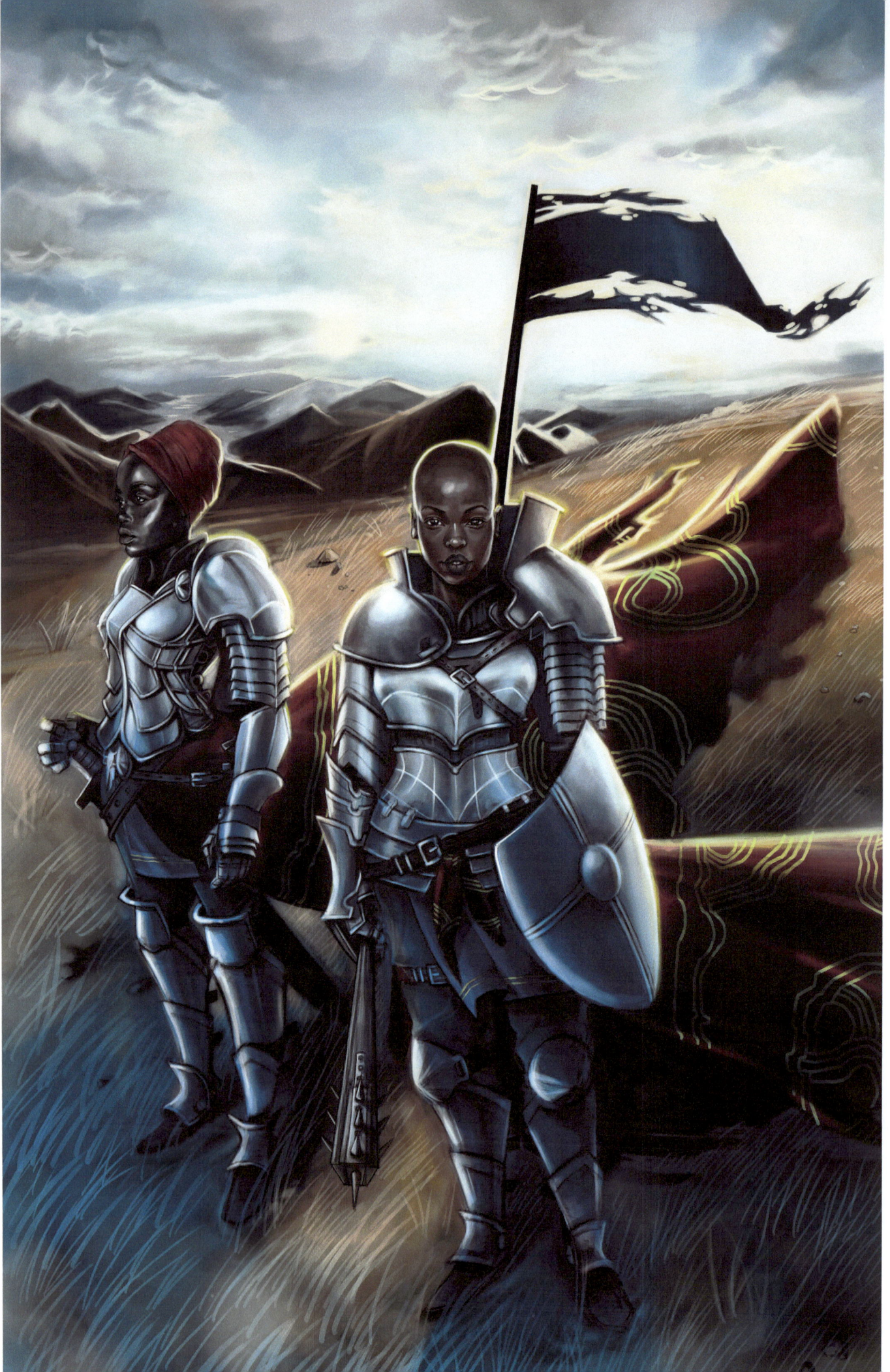

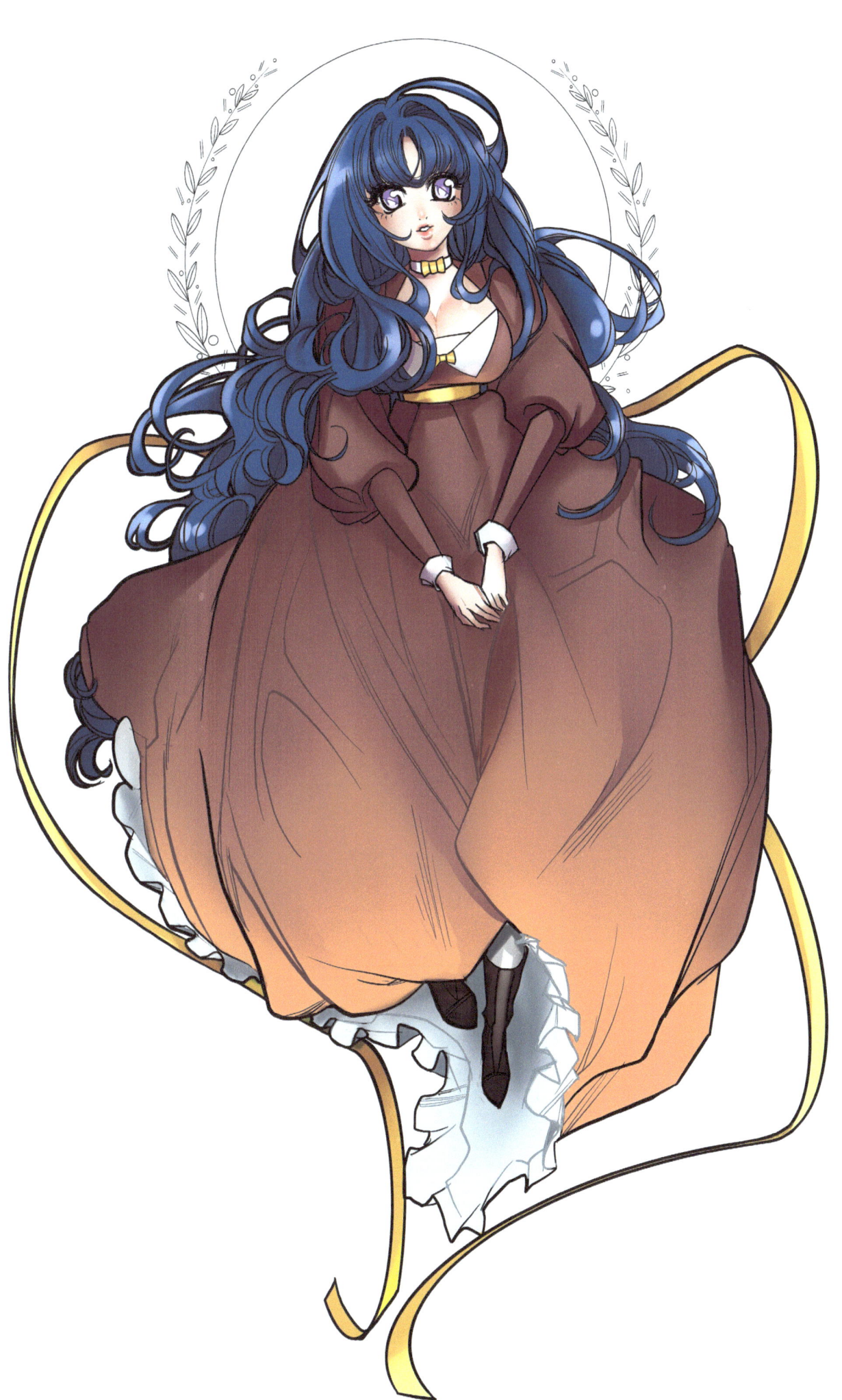

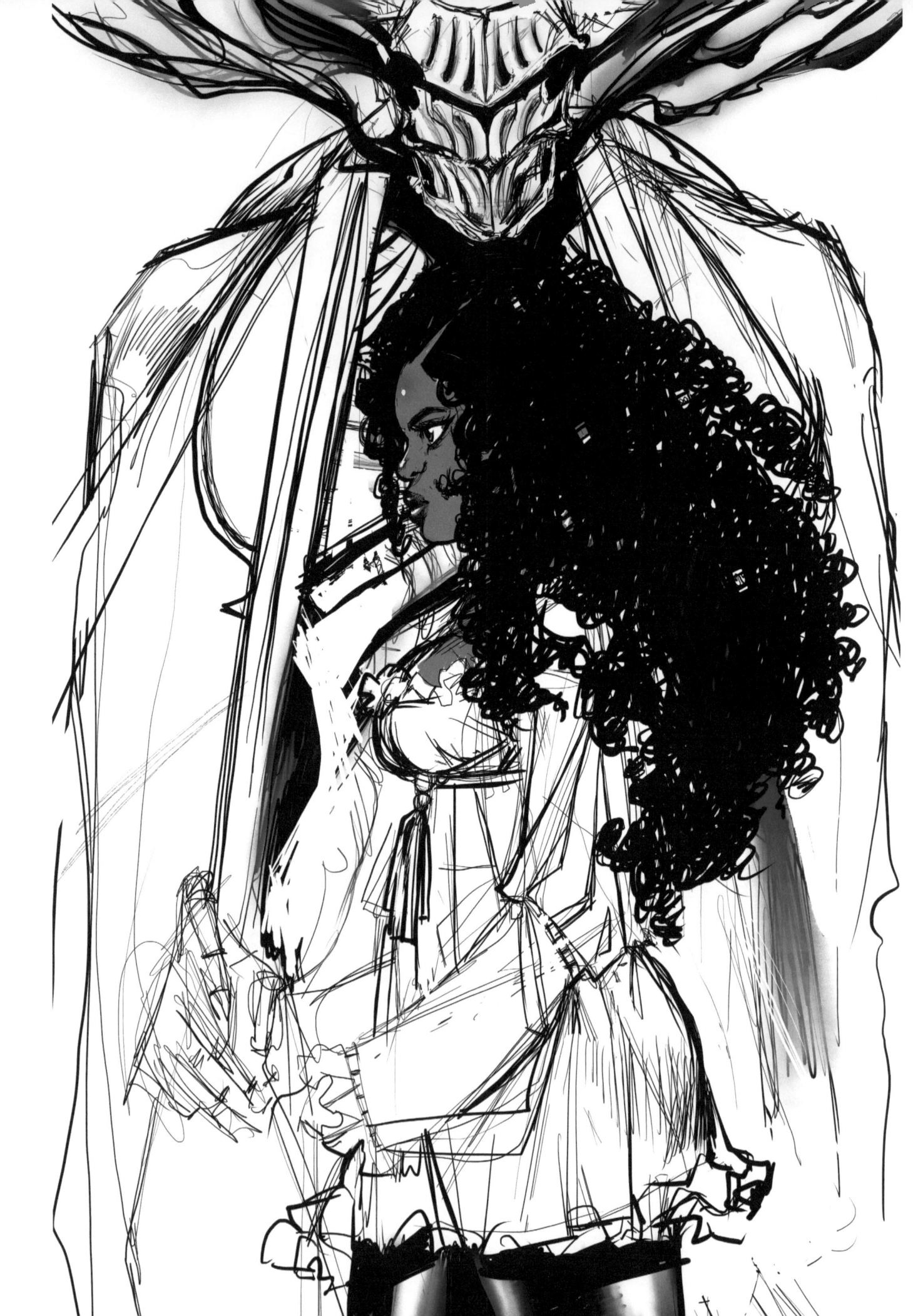

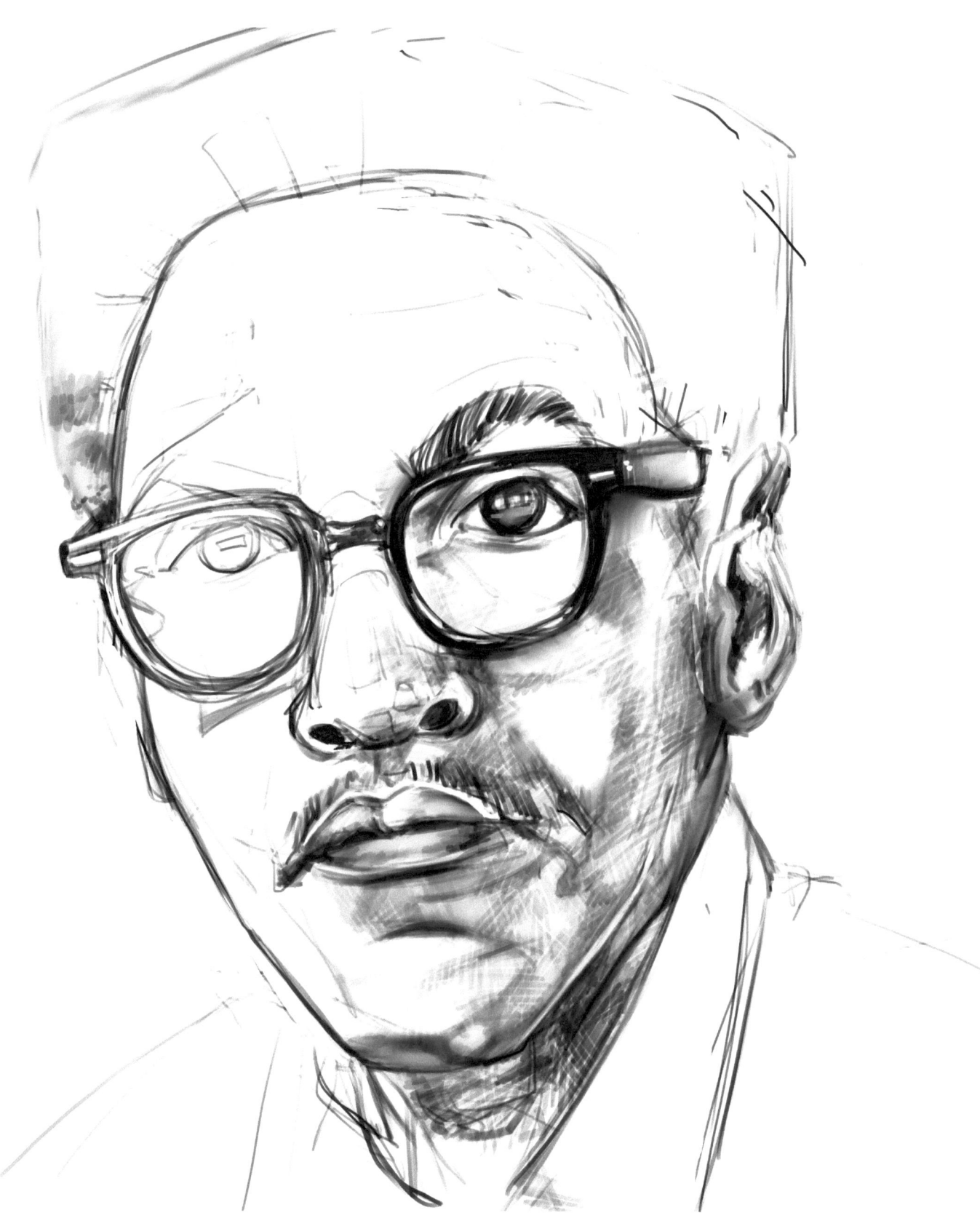

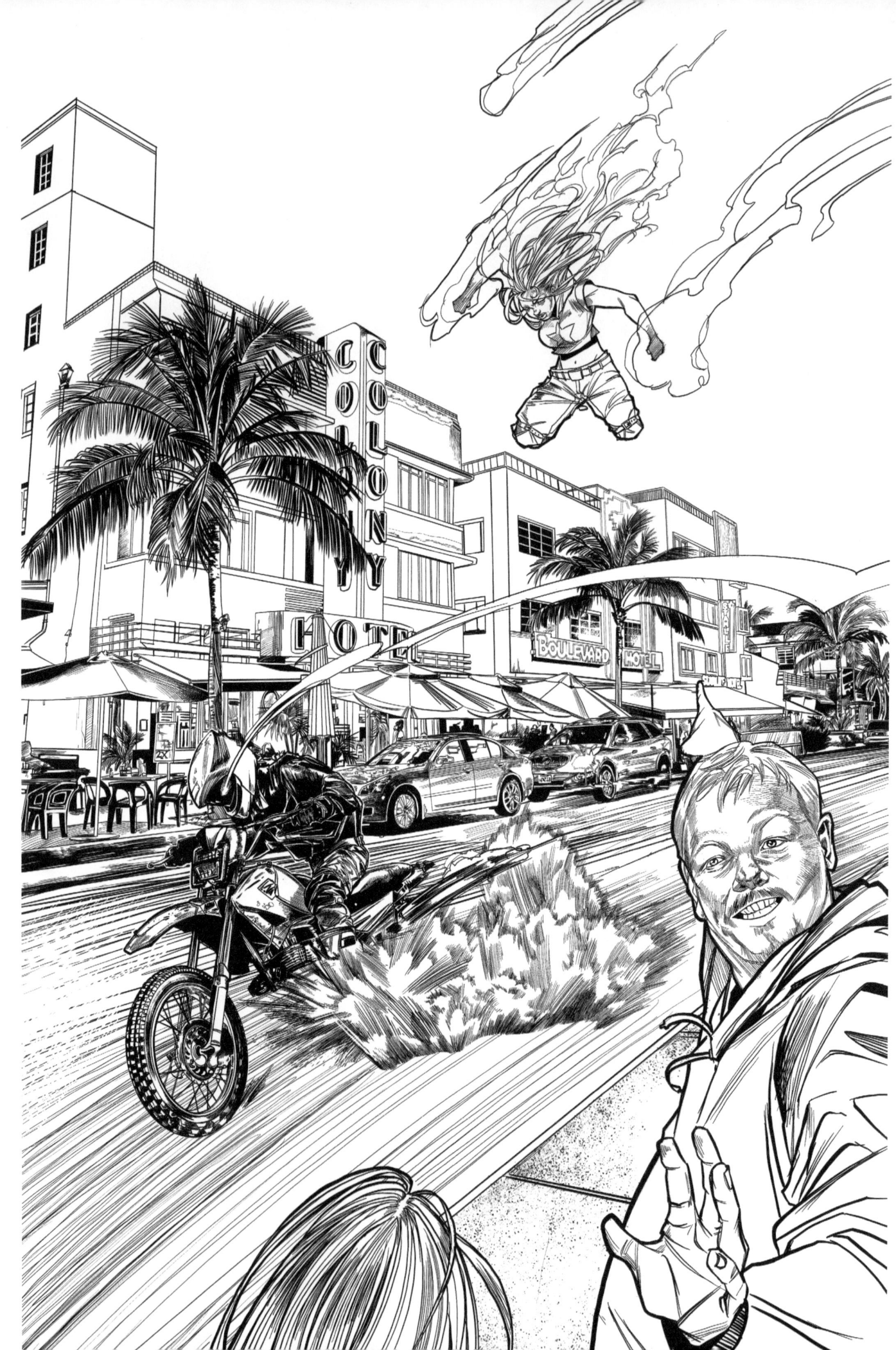

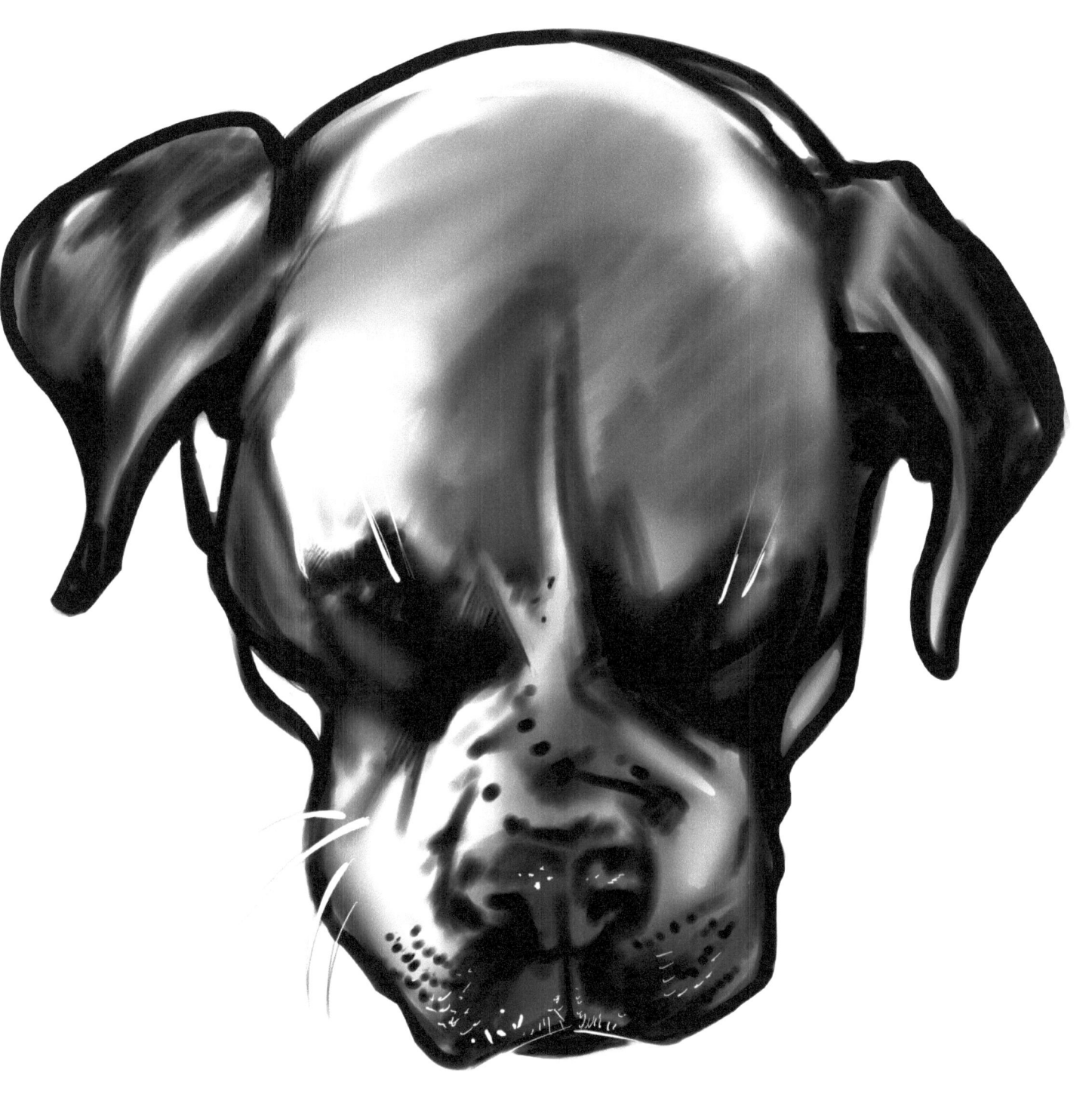

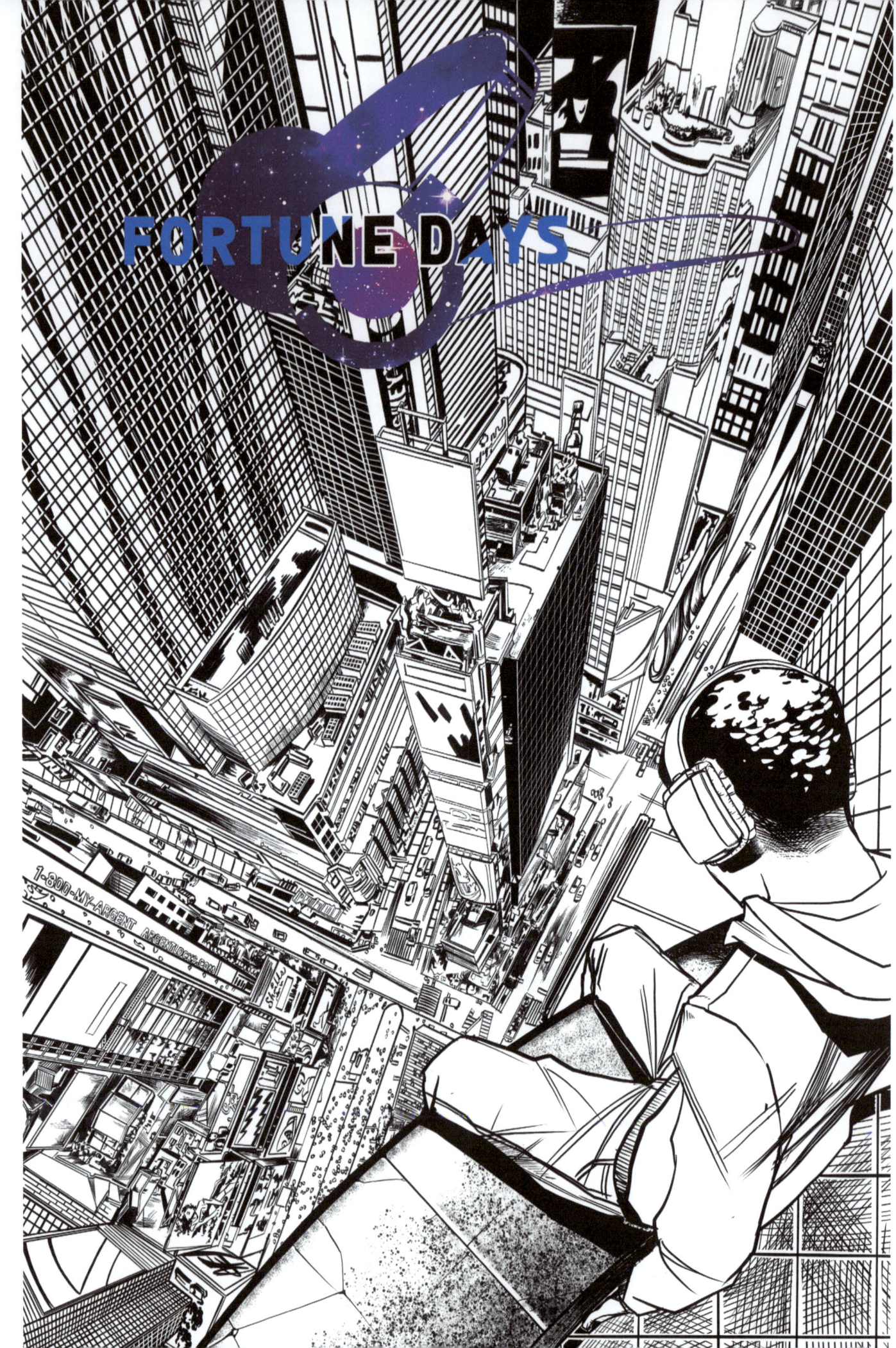

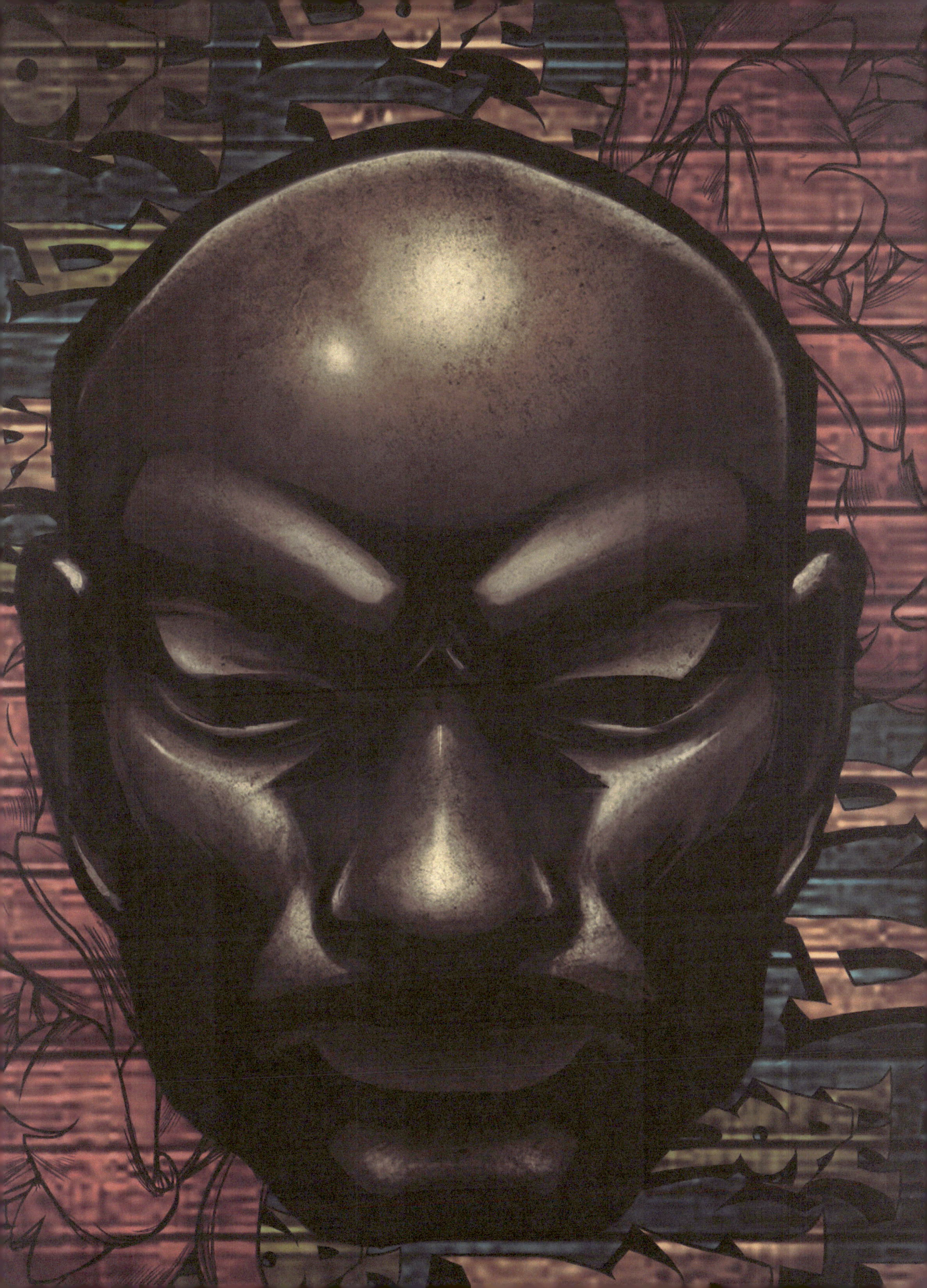

www.ingramcontent.com/pod-product-compliance
Lightning Source LLC
Chambersburg PA
CBHW051214220526
45473CB00003B/1023